李白与杜甫

LI BAI & DU FU

An Advanced Reader of Chinese Language and Literature

ZU-YAN CHEN

CHENG & TSUI COMPANY
BOSTON

17 16 15 14 13 12 11 10 09 08   1 2 3 4 5 6 7 8 9 10

Published by
Cheng & Tsui Company, Inc.
25 West Street
Boston, MA 02111-1213 USA
Fax (617) 426-3669
www.cheng-tsui.com
"Bringing Asia to the World"™

Simplified Character Edition
ISBN 978-0-88727-537-1

Library of Congress Cataloging-in-Publication Data

Chen, Zu-yan
    Li Bai & Du Fu : an advanced reader of Chinese language and literature = [Li Bai yu Du Fu] / by Zu-yan Chen.
        p. cm. -- (Cheng & Tsui Chinese literature series)
    Parallel title in Chinese characters.
    ISBN 978-0-88727-537-1
    1. Chinese language--Readers. 2. Chinese language--Textbooks for foreign speakers--English. 3. Li, Bai, 701-762--Criticism and interpretation. 4. Du, Fu, 712-770--Criticism and interpretation. I. Title. II. Title: Li Bai and Du Fu. III. Title: Li Bai yu Du Fu. IV. Series.

    PL1117.C39 2007
    495.1'86421--dc22

                                                    2007062022

Audio recordings of the poems in this volume are available at www.cheng-tsui.com.

Printed in the United States of America

Publisher's Note

The Cheng & Tsui Chinese Language Series is designed to publish and widely distribute quality language learning materials created by leading instructors from around the world. We welcome readers' comments and suggestions concerning the publications in this series. Please contact the following members of our Editorial Board, in care of our Editorial Department (e-mail: **editor@cheng-tsui.com**).

Cheng & Tsui Chinese Classics and Titles of Related Interest

Guanzi
Volume 1: Political, Economic and Philosophical Essays from Early China
W. Allyn Rickett
ISBN: 978-088727-324-7

Tales & Traditions
Readings in Chinese Literature Series, Volume 1
Adapted by Yun Xiao, Hui Xiao, and Ying Wang
ISBN: 978-0-88727-534-0

How Far Away Is the Sun?
And Other Essays
Readings in Chinese Culture Series, Volume 2
Weijia Huang and Qun Ao
ISBN: 978-088727-535-7

A Dream of Red Mansions
By Hsueh-chin Tsao; Translated by Ngo Kao, Hsien-Yi Yang, and Gladys Yang
ISBN: 978-088727-178-6

Midnight
By Mao Tun; Translated by A. C. Barnes and Meng-Hsiung Hsu
ISBN: 978-088727-099-4

The Way of Chinese Characters
The Origins of 400 Essential Words
By Jianhsin Wu; Illustrated by Chen Zheng and Chen Tian
ISBN: 978-0-88727-527-2

See **www.cheng-tsui.com** for more information about these and other titles of interest to Chinese language learners.

Contents

The Poetry of Du Fu   杜甫诗

Preface

This book represents an innovative approach to teaching Chinese language and literature at the advanced levels, featuring three combinations: those of classical and modern Chinese, language and literature, and poetry and prose. This innovation, however, is essentially a return to a Chinese tradition of poetry as a centerpiece of education and an underpinning of pedagogy. China is a nation of songbirds; the practice of memorizing and reciting poems stretches back to classical antiquity, when it was discovered that words and sounds—and the metrics by which they were bound together in poetry—awaken the mind and teach the language. Confucius (551–479 BCE) compiled the *Classic of Poetry* (*Shijing* 诗经), the first poetic anthology in China, and instructed his son: "If you do not study poetry, you will have no words"—"不学诗,无以言" (*Analects* XVI, 13). This close relationship between poetry and language was reflected by the fact that poetry served as a primer for literacy as well as one of the major subjects in the civil service examinations during the long course of Chinese history. Even in modern times, many children learn poems of the Tang Dynasty (618–907 CE) by heart long before they start formal schooling, where classical poems appear in the textbooks for all grades. This conviction of poetry's important function beyond pure entertainment is also shared in other cultures, as evidenced, for example, by English-speaking children's similar paths in learning, progressing from Dr. Seuss to William Shakespeare.

This universal practice of poetry as a tool for learning language and literature is indeed pedagogically sound. Students who study classical poetry learn a wide range of descriptive words that rarely appear in prose reading. This vocabulary, at once subtle and copious, heightens students' feel for the intricacies and complexities of the Chinese language—an indispensable asset if they are to go on to speak, write, and read Chinese with ease. Classical verse teaches an enormous amount about order, measure, proportion, correspondence, balance, symmetry, agreement, temporal relation, and contingent possibility. Mastering these concepts involves the most fundamental kind of learning, for these are the basic categories of thought and the framework in which we organize sensory experience. Furthermore, though usually more compact than prose, poetry makes intensive use of literary devices such as metaphor and allusion to enrich its interpretation.

In order to provide students with the best examples of poetic concepts of visualization, refinement, and cadence, this book concentrates on poems by Li Bai 李白 (701–762 CE) and Du Fu 杜甫 (712–770 CE), two of the brightest stars in China's poetic galaxy. With distinct styles, these two poets fostered a pithy expression of Chinese culture's accumulated wisdom. Even today, in the conversation of the educated, a quotation from Li or Du can speak volumes. The fourteen poems by Li and twelve poems by Du in this book belong in the repertoire of any well-educated Chinese speaker. These works, while arranged in five thematic categories, each stand as a separate chapter. Including the chapters on background information, the two poets' biographies, and short introductions to each thematic category, this book contains thirty-six chapters in total.

One distinct feature of this book is its "dual texts" system: Each poem is followed by a short essay of Analysis and Appreciation (赏析), which discusses the poem's linguistic, historical, literary, and philosophical aspects. These two texts of language and literature, one classical poetry and the other contemporary prose, contribute to the three combinations mentioned in the beginning of this Preface. Accordingly, each chapter contains two vocabulary lists: one for the poem and the other for Analysis and Appreciation. Together, the two texts deliver unique cognitive benefits, a sense of poetry, and a heightened feel for the language. Students who study these texts will be able to internalize the rhythmic, beautiful patterns of the Chinese language. These patterns will become part of the student's "language repertoire" that we all use for everyday writing and speaking.

To maximize the usefulness of this book, an effective method is memorization and recitation. Audio recordings of the poems included here are available at www.cheng-tsui.com. Students should listen carefully to the recordings and pay special attention to the pronunciation and cadence of the speaker's voice. Poetry memorization has become a dying art in most quarters. It is no longer emphasized and, in fact, strongly discouraged in most modern school curricula. Are exercises in memorizing and reciting poetry an archaic curiosity, without educative value? Students in the Li Bai and Du Fu course at Binghamton University would answer with a resounding "No!" They are required to memorize poems up to eight lines, and recitation—both solo and in chorus—is a daily practice. This exercise has demonstrated that memorizing and reciting poems is a great way to develop both a tenacious attention to detail and the essential literary skills that are key to critical thinking and unlocking the secrets of poetry. When one memorizes a poem, it is no longer just *a* poem, but *his* or *her* poem. When reciting it, students can practice varying the sounds, adding pauses and emphases in different spots in searching for the most accurate articulation for the poem.

Another pedagogical suggestion is dramatization and improvisation of some of the poems. Creating drama with poetry employs a multi-sensory approach to language acquisition by involving students physically, emotionally, and cognitively in the language learning process. Poems that express strong emotions, attitudes, feelings, opinions, or ideas are usually more "productive" than those which are gentle, descriptive, or neutral. In this book, for example, Du Fu's "The Officers of Shihao Village" (石壕吏) and "Newlyweds' Farewell" (新婚别) serve as good examples for dramatization because they are written in the form of monologues (or dialogue disguised as monologue) and have one simple but strong emotional theme. Students become engaged in free-flowing extemporaneous conversations as they interact with one another prior to the dramatizations and during the improvisations. They compare and contrast cultural behaviors and attitudes, analyze and explore the linguistic and conceptual differences between the poetic and spoken words, and interact cooperatively to orchestrate the dramatizations and improvisations.

The Exercises part of each chapter contains seven sections with different functions. The Multiple Choice (选择题) and Making Sentences (造句) sections offer vocabulary exercises, with a focus on the subtle differences between word choices. The Comprehension Questions (回答题) and Discussion Questions (讨论题) function as reviews of the texts. While the questions in the former are simple and straightforward, those in the latter are broad and comprehensive. The Translations from English into Chinese (英译中) and Translations from Chinese into English (中译英) sections provide translation training that is important to students at advanced levels. Finally, each chapter has a section of either Composition (作文) or Topic Research (专题研究). The latter provides students with a relevant topic to research, using the Internet and/or libraries. These research projects, although brief in nature and limited in scope, will challenge students to check information and resources in Chinese and English, and to report on their findings in Chinese.

Acknowledgments

This book is the result of a course with the same name, Li Bai and Du Fu, which I created at Binghamton University in 2005. In its two initial offerings, I posted course materials lesson by lesson on the university Blackboard™ system for students to print as handouts. My thanks thus first go to the students of these two classes who tolerated the inconvenience and incompletion of the virtual version of this book.

I am also indebted to Jenny Chen, who not only served as my teaching assistant for the 2006 class, but also helped me with my work on this volume. She read over the manuscript, made the Vocabulary Index and Proper Names Index, and converted the original simplified character text into the traditional character edition. It is most gratifying to see that her interest in Chinese literature has led her onto a track of teaching Chinese language and culture, and I wish her the best in her future career.

It gives me special pleasure to acknowledge my appreciation for the others who worked on *Li Bai & Du Fu*. Vivian Ling carefully edited the manuscript, purging it of inconsistencies, inaccuracies, and infelicities. Linda Robertson designed an innovative, artistic, and eye-catching cover. At Cheng & Tsui, Eleise Jones worked meticulously on the interior layout, making the book look fresh and functional; and Kristen Wanner coordinated the editing and production with expertise, efficiency, and enthusiasm. Together, they strengthened this volume immeasurably and expedited the publishing process.

Last but not the least, I would like to thank my wife and colleague Hong Zhang, to whom I owe double debts. Her unfailing encouragement and support made it possible for me to develop the course and book in a relatively short period of time. She also recited the poems and took on the technical challenges in making the accompanying audio recordings. I am sure that her voice will help students better appreciate the poems' powerful language and ideas and to develop their own minds and imaginations.

ZYC
June 2007

A note on the cover design: The phoenix design on the cover was inspired by two poetic lines: Li Bai's "the phoenix wandered over the Phoenix Terrace" (凤凰台上凤凰游) and Du Fu's "the phoenix grew old perching on the green Paulownia branches" (碧梧栖老凤凰枝).

1

Historical Background:
The An Lushan Rebellion
历史背景：安史之乱

词汇一

1. **安史之乱**, Ān Shǐ zhī luàn: The An Lushan (and Shi Siming) Rebellion
2. **盛**, shèng: flourishing, prosperous
3. **衰落**, shuāiluò: declining
4. **转折**, zhuǎnzhé: a turn in the course of events
5. **唐玄宗**, Táng Xuánzōng: Emperor Xuanzong of the Tang (r. 712–56)
6. **顶峰**, dǐngfēng: peak
7. **作为**, zuòwéi: accomplishment
8. **贵妃**, guìfēi: Precious Concubine (a high-ranking imperial concubine)
9. **理**, lǐ: to manage, to run
10. **朝政**, cháozhèng: government affairs
11. **重用**, zhòngyòng: to put somebody in an important position
12. **安禄山**, Ān Lùshān: the head of the rebellion
13. **边境**, biānjìng: border, frontier
14. **起兵**, qǐbīng: to rise in arms, to start military action
15. **造反**, zàofǎn: to rebel, to revolt
16. **副手**, fùshǒu: lieutenant, assistant
17. **史思明**, Shǐ Sīmíng: An Lushan's lieutenant (d. 761)
18. **叛军**, pànjūn: rebellious army
19. **次年**, cìnián: following year
20. **长安**, Cháng'ān: Capital of the Tang Dynasty, today's Xi'an 西安
21. **仓皇**, cānghuáng: in a flurry, in panic
22. **持续**, chíxù: to continue
23. **平定**, píngdìng: to suppress, to put down (a rebellion)
24. **军阀**, jūnfá: warlord
25. **混战**, hùnzhàn: tangled warfare
26. **局面**, júmiàn: situation, phase
27. **衰亡**, shuāiwáng: decline and destruction
28. **风格**, fēnggé: style
29. **爆发**, bàofā: to erupt, to burst out, to break out
30. **描绘**, miáohuì: to depict, to describe

历史背景：安史之乱

　　李白和杜甫的时代，是唐朝从全盛到衰落的转折时期。

　　唐朝的政治、经济和文化在唐玄宗时都发展到了顶峰。年轻时很有作为的唐玄宗，年老时渐渐地骄傲起来。他爱上了一个姓杨的贵妃，从此不理朝政，并且重用坏人。公元七五五年，一个名叫安禄山的将军在东北部边境起兵造反。安禄山的副手叫史思明，所以这场叛乱就叫做"安史之乱"。叛军次年攻下首都长安，玄宗仓皇逃到四川。安史之乱持续了八年，对社会的破坏很大。叛乱平定以后，军阀混战的局面又开始形成，唐朝从此走向衰亡。

　　李白比杜甫大十一岁，这十一年与他们两人的不同的人生道路和诗歌风格有很大的关系。安史之乱爆发时李白五十四岁，之后又生活了七年。他的大部分诗作是在战乱前写的，反映了唐朝积极向上的精神。杜甫在七五五年时四十三岁，之后又生活了十五年。他写了大量描绘战争的破坏和人民的苦难的诗篇。

练习

一、选择题

1. 李白和杜甫的时代是唐朝的 _____ 时期。
   - a. 全盛
   - (b.) 衰落
   - c. 转折
   - d. 顶峰

2. 唐朝的 _____ 在唐玄宗时都发展到了顶峰。
   - a. 政治
   - b. 经济
   - c. 文化
   - (d.) 政治、经济和文化

3. 唐玄宗不理朝政是因为他 _____ 。
   - a. 年老
   - b. 没有作为
   - c. 安禄山叛乱
   - (d.) 爱上了杨贵妃

4. 公元七五五年，安禄山在 _____ 部边境起兵造反。
   - (a.) 东北
   - b. 西北
   - c. 东南
   - d. 西南

5. 安禄山攻下长安后，唐玄宗仓皇逃到 _____ 。
   - (a.) 四川
   - b. 西安
   - c. 长安
   - d. 北京

6. 安史之乱持续了 _____ 年。
   - a. 七
   - (b.) 八
   - c. 十一
   - d. 十五

二、造句

1. 衰落　　2. 转折　　3. 顶峰　　4. 作为　　5. 持续
6. 局面　　7. 风格　　8. 描绘

三、中译英

1. 唐朝是中国诗歌的黄金时代，现存的唐诗有五万多首。
2. 北京是元、明、清等朝代的国都，西安作过秦、汉、唐等朝代的国都。
3. 唐朝诗人白居易的长诗《长恨歌》写的就是唐玄宗和杨贵妃的爱情故事。

4. 唐朝时经过中亚到欧洲的通商的道路叫做"丝绸之路"。

四、英译中

1. The time of Li Bai and Du Fu was a turning point for the Tang Dynasty from grandeur to decline.
2. Li Bai was eleven years older than Du Fu. These eleven years were a determining factor in the different life paths and poetic styles of these two poets.
3. Li Bai wrote most of his poems before the rebellion, reflecting the vigorous spirit of the Tang Dynasty.
4. Du Fu wrote many poems describing the destruction and people's misfortunes caused by the war.

五、回答题

1. 唐朝的政治、经济和文化在哪个皇帝的时候发展到了顶峰？
2. 唐玄宗在年轻时和年老时有什么不同？
3. 唐朝的首都叫什么？现在叫什么？
4. 安禄山是在哪儿起兵造反的？
5. 为什么这次叛乱叫安史之乱？

六、讨论题

1. 安史之乱对唐朝历史有什么影响？
2. 李白比杜甫大几岁？这个年龄差别对他们的诗歌创作有什么影响？

七、专题研究

1. 唐玄宗和杨贵妃的爱情故事。（关键词：唐玄宗、杨贵妃、华清池、马嵬坡、长恨歌）

2

Philosophical Background: Confucianism and Daoism

哲学背景：儒家与道家

词汇一

1. **儒家**, Rújiā: Confucianism
2. **道家**, Dàojiā: Daoism (Taoism)
3. **孔子**, Kǒngzi: Confucius (551–479 BCE)
4. **流派**, liúpài: schools (of thought, art, etc.)
5. **创始人**, chuàngshǐrén: founder
6. **学派**, xuépài: schools (of learning, thought)
7. **强调**, qiángdiào: to emphasize
8. **老子**, Lǎozi: Laozi
9. **着眼**, zhuóyǎn: to pay attention to
10. **于**, yú: 在
11. **宇宙**, yǔzhòu: universe, cosmos
12. **建功立业**, jiàngōng lìyè: to earn merit and accomplish a great deal in one's career
13. **顺应**, shùnyìng: to comply with
14. **对立**, duìlì: in opposition, conflicting
15. **补充**, bǔchōng: complementary, supplementary
16. **人生观**, rénshēngguān: outlook on life
17. **倾向**, qīngxiàng: to be inclined to, to prefer
18. **幻想**, huànxiǎng: to cherish illusions, to imagine
19. **丑恶**, chǒu' è: ugly
20. **及时行乐**, jíshí xínglè: to make merry in a timely fashion
21. **主题**, zhǔtí: theme
22. **坚定**, jiāndìng: firm
23. **抱负**, bàofù: aspiration
24. **揭露**, jiēlù: to unmask, to expose
25. **矛盾**, máodùn: contradictory, contradiction
26. **称号**, chēnghào: title, name
27. **仙**, xiān: celestial, immortal
28. **圣**, shèng: sage
29. **含义**, hányì: meaning, implication
30. **追求**, zhuīqiú: to seek, to pursue
31. **境界**, jìngjiè: state, realm
32. **迥异**, jiǒngyì: distinctly different
33. **传诵**, chuánsòng: to be widely read, to be on everyone's lips
34. **千古**, qiāngǔ: through the ages

哲学背景：儒家与道家

中国传统哲学思想流派众多，其中最重要的是儒家与道家。以孔子为创始人的儒家学派强调道德、秩序和个人对社会的贡献。以老子学说为中心的道家着眼于人的精神自由以及人与宇宙的关系。儒家主张建功立业，道家希望顺应自然。这两种思想既是对立的，又是互相补充的。

李白与杜甫虽然是好友，人生观却有很大的不同。李白倾向于道家哲学。他幻想在自由的天地中生活，忘掉各种丑恶的社会现实。人生如梦和及时行乐是李白诗中常见的主题。杜甫是一个坚定的儒家学者。他希望能实现政治上的抱负。他的诗揭露社会矛盾，反映战乱中人民的痛苦生活。

正因为如此，后人给了李白和杜甫每人一个很有意思的称号：李白被称为"诗仙"，杜甫被称为"诗圣"。这两个称号首先是说明李、杜两人代表了中国诗歌艺术的最高成就，同时也有着哲学的含义。成仙是道家追求的境界，而圣人是儒家最高的理想。一仙一圣，成为最好的朋友，并写出了风格迥异却又同样传诵千古的诗篇。

练习

一、选择题

1. 儒家主张 _____ 。
   - a. 人生如梦
   - b. 及时行乐
   - c. 顺应自然
   - (d.) 建功立业

2. _____ 是李白诗中常见的主题。
   - a. 道德
   - b. 秩序
   - c. 自由
   - d. 贡献

3. 杜甫被后人称为 _____ 。
   - a. 诗仙
   - (b.) 诗圣
   - c. 诗佛
   - d. 诗鬼

4. 杜甫在他的诗中 _____ 人民的痛苦生活。
   - a. 强调
   - b. 揭露
   - c. 追求
   - (d.) 反映

二、造句

1. 强调　　2. 对立　　3. 幻想　　4. 主题　　5. 坚定
6. 抱负　　7. 揭露　　8. 矛盾　　9. 称号　　10. 含义
11. 追求

三、中译英

1. 中国最早的一本诗歌总集叫《诗经》，是孔子亲自编的。

2. 古代的人常常用写诗的方式来表达自己的哲学思想和人生观。

3. 一个人年轻时都想建功立业，年老了又往往会觉得人生如梦。

4. 虽然儒家和道家思想都很普遍，但在中国古代社会中占统治地位的是儒家思想。

四、英译中

1. Confucianism, which acknowledges Confucius as its founder, advocates morals, order, and individual contributions to society.
2. Daoism, centered on the teachings of Laozi, focused on individual freedom and man's place in the larger cosmic scheme.
3. Confucianism and Daoism are contradictory, yet also mutually complementary.
4. The poems by Li Bai and Du Fu represent the highest achievements in Chinese poetry; however, they reflect very different philosophical inclinations.

五、回答题

1. 中国传统哲学思想中最重要的是哪两家？
2. 儒家的创始人是谁？道家的创始人是谁？
3. 李白诗中有哪些常见的主题？

六、讨论题

1. 儒家思想和道家思想有什么不同？
2. 李白和杜甫的哲学思想有什么不同？对他们的诗歌创作有什么影响？
3. 为什么后人称李白为"诗仙"、杜甫为"诗圣"？

七、专题研究

1.《论语》是孔子的语录，《老子》是道家的经典。请你从这两本书中各找出一段你觉得有意义的话，给班上的同学做个介绍。

3

Literary Background:
Poetic Form
文学背景：诗歌格律

词汇一

1. **格律**, gélǜ: poetic regulations
2. **源远流长**, yuányuǎn liúcháng: a distant source and a long stream, of long standing, well-established
3. **完备**, wánbèi: complete
4. **押韵**, yāyùn: to rhyme
5. **对仗**, duìzhàng: parallelism (in poetry)
6. **声调**, shēngdiào: tones
7. **绝句**, juéjù: quatrain, a poem of four lines
8. **律诗**, lǜshī: regulated verse
9. **搭配**, dāpèi: to match up, to coordinate
10. **限制**, xiànzhì: restriction; to restrict
11. **联**, lián: (poetic) couplet
12. **大致**, dàzhì: generally, roughly
13. **词类**, cílèi: parts of speech (such as noun, verb, etc.)
14. **规定**, guīdìng: to prescribe, to formulate
15. **朗诵**, lǎngsòng: to recite (a poem, etc.)
16. **乐感**, yuègǎn: musical feeling
17. **复杂**, fùzá: complicated, complex
18. **体会**, tǐhuì: understanding (through direct personal experience)

文学背景：诗歌格律

中国的诗歌源远流长。到了唐代，诗歌格律就很完备了。诗歌格律主要包括以下几个方面：字数句数、押韵、对仗和声调。

首先是字数句数。每句五个字的叫五言诗，每句七个字的叫七言诗。一首诗四句的叫绝句，八句的叫律诗。搭配起来，就有了五言绝句、七言绝句、五言律诗、七言律诗。还有一些诗，句数比较多、写法比较自由、不受严格的格律限制的，叫古风；当然也分五言古风和七言古风。

中国古典诗歌都押韵。双数句必须押韵，第一句可押可不押，但多半也押韵。

律诗的中间两联应该是对句。大致来说，就是在一联中，位置相同的两个字应该词类相同，比如名词对名词（"天"对"地"），形容词对形容词（"红"对"黑"）。

比较难的是声调。古代也有四声，可是跟现代的四声不一样。格律诗的每个字都有规定的声调，因此在朗诵时给人以乐感。这个问题比较复杂，诗读得多了，慢慢会有点体会。

练习

一、选择题

1. 中国的诗歌格律到了 _____ 就很完备了。
   - a. 汉代
   - b. 唐代
   - c. 宋代
   - d. 明代
2. 一首八句、每句七个字的诗叫 _____ 。
   - a. 五言绝句
   - b. 七言绝句
   - c. 五言律诗
   - d. 七言律诗
3. 句数比较多、写法比较自由、不受格律限制的诗叫 _____ 。
   - a. 自由诗
   - b. 古风
   - c. 律诗
   - d. 绝句

二、造句

1. 源远流长　2. 完备　3. 搭配　4. 限制　5. 大致
6. 规定　7. 复杂　8. 体会

三、中译英

1. 中国诗歌格律和英文诗歌格律有很大的不同。
2. 如果你要写一首格律诗，你一定要按照所有的格律来写。
3. 要是你不愿意或不会写格律诗，你可以写自由体诗。
4. 写自由体诗可以很自由，可长可短，甚至可以不押韵。

四、英译中

1. Poetic regulations include the following aspects: the numbers of characters and lines, rhyme, parallelism, and tone patterns.
2. Rhyme is mandatory on even-numbered lines. The first line is optional, though usually also rhymed.
3. There were four tones in ancient times, but they are different from the four tones of modern times.
4. The tone for each character in regulated verse is prescribed; therefore, reciting a poem provides a sense of music.

5. This is a complex issue, but after one has studied many poems, one will gradually gain some understanding of the tones.

五、回答题

1. 诗歌格律主要包括哪几个方面?
2. 中国古典诗歌大致上是怎么押韵的?
3. 律诗中的哪两联应该是对句?

六、讨论题

1. 中国古典诗歌在形式上可分成哪六种? 请说说它们的字数句数规定。
2. 请讲一讲什么是对仗。

七、专题研究

1. 比较一下中国诗歌格律和英文诗歌格律。

A Brief Biography of Li Bai
李白小传

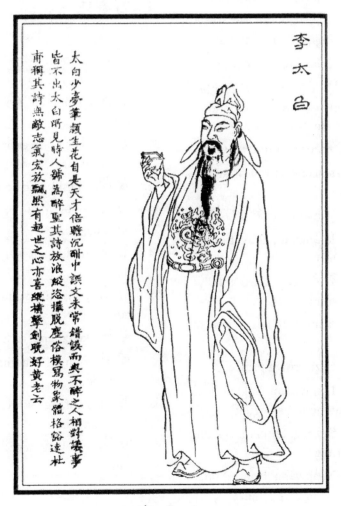

太白少夢筆頭生花自是天才倍贍沉酣中誤文未嘗錯誤而與不醉之人相對爭事
皆不出太白所見時人蹄為醉聖其詩放浪縱恣擺脫塵俗模寫物象體格舒遠杜
甫稱其詩無敵志氣宏放飄然有超世之心亦喜縱橫擊劍晚好黃老云

李太白

词汇一

1. 字, zì: courtesy name
2. 显露, xiǎnlù: to manifest
3. 才华, cáihuá: literary or artistic talent
4. 雄心壮志, xióngxīn zhuàngzhì: lofty aspirations
5. 漫游, mànyóu: roaming, wandering
6. 科举, kējǔ: civil service examinations (in imperial times)
7. 推荐, tuījiàn: to recommend
8. 征召, zhēngzhào: to summon
9. 翰林院, Hànlín Yuàn: Hanlin Academy (where literary and artistic talents were lodged)
10. 诏书, zhàoshū: imperial edict
11. 侍从, shìcóng: to follow and to serve
12. 宴游, yànyóu: 宴会和游览
13. 狂放, kuángfàng: unrestrained (character)
14. 格格不入, gégé búrù: totally incompatible
15. 陷落, xiànluò: to fall into enemy hands
16. 太子, tàizǐ: crown prince
17. 灵武, Língwǔ: in Ningxia 宁夏 Hui Autonomous Region
18. 肃宗, Sùzōng: Emperor Suzong of the Tang (r. 756–761)
19. 永王, Yǒngwáng: Prince Yong
20. 幕僚, mùliáo: close aide (to someone in high office)
21. 皇位, huángwèi: the throne
22. 逮捕, dàibǔ: to arrest
23. 判, pàn: to sentence
24. 流放, liúfàng: exile
25. 夜郎, Yèláng: in today's Guizhou 贵州 Province
26. 朝廷, cháotíng: imperial court, imperial government
27. 大赦, dàshè: amnesty
28. 白帝城, Báidì Chéng: in today's Sichuan 四川 Province
29. 漂泊, piāobó: to lead a wandering life
30. 当涂, Dāngtú: in Anhui 安徽 Province
31. 鹏, péng: roc (an enormous, mythical bird of prey)
32. 蔑视, mièshì: to disdain
33. 权贵, quánguì: powerful high officials
34. 否定, fǒudìng: to negate, to renounce
35. 功名, gōngmíng: official positions
36. 夸张, kuāzhāng: exaggeration
37. 雄奇, xióngqí: magnificent and marvelous
38. 奔放, bēnfàng: expressive and untrammeled
39. 飘逸, piāoyì: graceful and natural

A Brief Biography of Li Bai

李白小传

李白（701-762），字太白。他在四川长大，少年时即显露才华和雄心壮志。二十三岁离开家乡，长期在各地漫游。他没有像他的同时代人一样通过科举考试来取得政府中的官职。

李白四十一岁时，由于朋友的推荐，被唐玄宗征召进京，并授予翰林院学士的职称。在长安，李白起草诏书，侍从宴游，创作诗篇。但是他的狂放的性格和朝廷的生活格格不入，因此在长安生活了不到两年就被迫离开了。在此后的漫游中， 李白遇到了杜甫。两人结下了深厚的情谊。

公元七五五年，安禄山叛乱。长安陷落后，玄宗逃往四川。太子在灵武作了皇帝，史称肃宗。玄宗的另外一个儿子永王在东南组织抵抗，请李白参加他的军队。李白满怀报国热情，作了他的幕僚。肃宗怀疑永王想跟他争夺皇位，因此派兵打败了永王。李白也被逮捕，并被判流放夜郎。公元七五九年，朝廷发布大赦令，李白在流放途中的白帝城获释。李白晚年漂泊困苦，六十一岁时在当涂病死。

李白现存诗一千多首。他经常以大鹏自喻，对自己的才能充满信心。他的不少诗篇表现了蔑视权贵、否定功名的思想。他的诗以丰富的想象、极度的夸张以及生动的比喻为特色，形成一种雄奇、奔放、飘逸的风格。

练习

一、选择题

1. 安禄山叛乱时，李白 _____ 岁。
   a. 二十三　　　　　b. 四十一
   c. 五十四　　　　　d. 六十一

2. 李白在晚年被流放到 _____ 。
   a. 灵武　　　　　　b. 夜郎
   c. 白帝城　　　　　d. 当涂

3. 李白的不少诗篇表现了 _____ 权贵的思想。
   a. 怀疑　　　　　　b. 妒嫉
   c. 诬蔑　　　　　　d. 蔑视

4. 李白的诗中充满 _____ 的想象。
   a. 夸张　　　　　　b. 奔放
   c. 丰富　　　　　　d. 狂放

二、造句

1. 才华　　2. 雄心壮志　3. 推荐　　　4. 逮捕　　　5. 判
6. 否定　　7. 夸张　　　8. 奔放

三、中译英

1. 李白是中国文学史上少见的天才。他的诗被中国人民千古传诵。

2. 李白的诗被翻译成英文、法文、德文、俄文、日文等很多种语文。世界各国都有李白诗歌的爱好者和研究者。

3. 李白的一生，经历很丰富，留下了很多有趣的故事和传说。

4. 唐朝的音乐、舞蹈、书法、绘画都很发达，这些艺术对李白的诗歌创作都有很大的影响。

四、英译中

1. Li Bai never took the civil service examinations as his contemporaries did, though that was the normal route to a career in government.
2. Li Bai received a summons by Emperor Xuanzong that took him to the capital. He was appointed a scholar in the Hanlin Academy.
3. On his way to exile in 759, Li Bai was freed by imperial amnesty in the City of Baidi.
4. His poems touch readers' hearts with rich imagination, extreme exaggeration, and vivid metaphor, and are presented in a uniquely magnificent, untrammeled, and graceful style.

五、回答题

1. 李白的字是什么？他在哪儿长大？
2. 李白有没有参加过科举考试？
3. 李白是怎么进京当上翰林学士的？他在长安做些什么？
4. 李白为什么离开了长安？
5. 李白参加了谁的军队？为什么？
6. 李白为什么被流放？他在哪里得到大赦？
7. 李白晚年的生活怎么样？
8. 李白现存诗歌有多少首？
9. 李白把自己比作什么？为什么？

六、讨论题

1. 请你说一说李白的一生。
2. 请你介绍李白诗歌的风格。

七、专题研究

1. "杨国忠磨墨、高力士脱靴"的故事。

5

A Brief Introduction to
Moon Poetry
咏月诗小序

青天有月来几时，我今停杯一问之。人攀明月不可得，月行却与人相随。皎如飞镜临丹阙，绿烟灭尽清辉发。但见宵从海上来，宁知晓向云间没。白兔捣药秋复春，嫦娥孤栖与谁邻。今人不见古时月，今月曾经照古人。古人今人若流水，共看明月皆如此。唯愿当歌对酒时，月光长照金樽里。

临华喜昌书太白把酒问月诗

把酒问月

词汇一

1. **咏**, yǒng: to chant, to recite (a poem)
2. **疑**, yí: to suspect
3. **瑶台**, Yáotái: Jade Terrace, an abode of fairies in Chinese mythology
4. **端**, duān, end
5. **朗**, lǎng: bright
6. **行**, xíng: an ancient poetic form
7. **晶莹**, jīngyíng: glittering and crystal-clear
8. **皎洁**, jiǎojié: (of moonlight) white and clear
9. **染**, rǎn: to dye, to contaminate
10. **攀**, pān: to climb
11. **象征**, xiàngzhēng: symbol
12. **清净**, qīngjìng: peaceful and quiet
13. **神奇**, shénqí: magical, miraculous
14. **烦恼**, fánnǎo: vexation, worries
15. **淡化**, dànhuà: to lighten, to lessen
16. **心灵**, xīnlíng: heart, soul
17. **翱翔**, áoxiáng: to hover, to soar
18. **钟情**, zhōngqíng: to be deeply in love
19. **永恒**, yǒnghéng: eternity
20. **短暂**, duǎnzàn: short duration, transience
21. **变迁**, biànqiān: changes, vicissitudes
22. **观察**, guānchá: to observe
23. **探索**, tànsuǒ: to explore
24. **奥秘**, àomì: profound mystery

小序

　　李白非常喜爱明月。他从小就对月亮有兴趣："小时不识月，呼作白玉盘。又疑瑶台镜，飞在青云端"（《古朗月行》）。李白现存的一千多首诗中，写到月亮的就有三百八十二首，占百分之三十八。

　　李白为什么如此爱月亮呢？因为月亮晶莹皎洁、一尘不染、高不可攀，是光明的象征，是美好事物的代表。月光下的天地，是一个清净的和神奇的理想世界。一切人世间的烦恼都被月光淡化了。诗人的心灵可以在广阔的月空中自由翱翔。

　　李白之所以对月亮如此之钟情，还因为明月象征着永恒。月亮高高在上，把人生的短暂、人世的变迁都观察得清清楚楚。如果你想探索人生的意义和宇宙的奥秘，是不是能从月亮的光辉中找到一些答案呢？

练习

一、选择题

1. 月亮晶莹 _____ 、一尘不染、高不可攀，是光明的象征。

        a. 雪白   **b.** 光明

        c. 清洁   **d.** 皎洁

2. 月亮高高在上，把人生的短暂、人世的变迁都观察得 _____ 。

        a. 清清楚楚   **b.** 明明白白

        c. 干干净净   **d.** 整整齐齐

3. 如果你想 _____ 人生的意义和宇宙的奥秘，你是不是能从月亮的光辉中找到一些答案呢？

        a. 掌握   **b.** 注意

        c. 观察   **d.** 探索

二、造句

1. 皎洁   2. 象征   3. 钟情   4. 永恒   5. 短暂

6. 变迁   7. 探   8. 奥秘

三、中译英

1. 小时不识月，呼作白玉盘。又疑瑶台镜，飞在青云端。

2. 在唐诗中，月亮有许多美丽的代称，如：天镜、玉盘、玉兔、冰轮、圆光等，都很形象，很有诗意。

3. 唐诗中有许多咏月诗，除了李白的诗以外，张若虚写的《春江花月夜》也非常有名。

4. 李白常常把月亮跟其他景物一起描写，如：星月、云月、风月、花月、松月、霜月、山月、水月等，真是丰富多彩、美不胜收。

四、英译中

1. Another reason why Li Bai was so deeply fond of the moon was because it symbolized eternity.
2. If you want to explore life's meaning and the secret of the cosmos, you may find some answers from the radiance of the moon.
3. The poet's soul can soar freely in the vast, moonlit sky.
4. The moon sees clearly the transience of human life and the vicissitudes of the human world.

五、回答题

1. 李白小时候把月亮叫做什么？在他的想象中，月亮成了什么？
2. 李白诗中写到月亮的诗占百分之几？

六、讨论题

1. 从月亮象征光明和永恒这两个方面来谈谈李白为什么对月亮如此钟情。

七、专题研究

1. 介绍一下中秋节。（关键词：中秋节、赏月、月饼、中秋诗词）

6

Thoughts on a Still Night
静夜思

词汇一

1. **霜**, shuāng: frost
2. **举**, jǔ: to lift, to raise

静夜思

床前明月光，疑是地上霜。
举头望明月，低头思故乡。

赏析

中国有一个传统：往往在孩子很小的时候，父母就教孩子背唐诗。很多孩子背的第一首诗就是这首《静夜思》。这可能是因为这首诗很短，用词也很简单，但更主要的是这首诗生动地写出了思念家乡的感情。

古代交通很不方便，所以旅行在外常会有强烈的思乡之情。圆月象征团圆，更会激发这种情感。

月白霜清，是秋天夜景。诗人夜半醒来，看到床前地上一片月色，以为是浓霜。他抬头看到山头的明月，勾起了一片乡愁。短短四句诗，写得明白如话。它的内容是单纯的，但同时又是丰富的；它是容易理解的，却又是体味不尽的。从这首诗，我们不难体会到李白诗的清新自然的本色。

词汇二

1. **生动**, shēngdòng: lively, vividly
2. **团圆**, tuányuán: family reunion
3. **激发**, jīfā: to arouse, to stimulate
4. **勾**, gōu: to induce, to evoke
5. **乡愁**, xiāngchóu: homesickness, nostalgia
6. **单纯**, dānchún: simple, pure
7. **却**, què: but, yet
8. **体味**, tǐwèi: to appreciate, to savor
9. **尽**, jìn: exhausted, finished
10. **清新**, qīngxīn: pure and fresh
11. **本色**, běnsè: original color, true quality

练习

一、选择题

1. 中国有一个 _____ ：往往在孩子很小的时候，
父母就教孩子背唐诗。

      a. 风俗   **b.** 习惯

      c. 传统   **d.** 传说

2. 这首诗 _____ 地写出了思念家乡的感情。

      a. 生动   **b.** 活泼

      c. 清新   **d.** 单纯

3. 圆月 _____ 团圆，更会激发这种情感。

      a. 比喻   **b.** 象征

      c. 说明   **d.** 解释

4. 从这首诗，我们不难 _____ 到李白诗的清新
自然的本色。

      a. 体察   **b.** 体会

      c. 体验   **d.** 体现

二、造句

1. 生动   2. 团圆   3. 激发   4. 乡愁   5. 单纯

6. 体会   7. 清新   8. 本色

三、中译英

1. 床前明月光，疑是地上霜。举头望明月，低头思故乡。

2. 中国人旅行在外，看到月亮往往会思念故乡，可能跟这
首诗有关系吧。

3. 从这首诗我们可以体会到，好诗常常是很自然、很简
单的。

4. 这首诗的内容是单纯的，但同时又是丰富的；它是容易
理解的，却又是体味不尽的。

四、英译中

1. There is a tradition in China, that parents teach their children to memorize and recite Tang poems when they are very young.
2. Because transportation was very inconvenient in ancient times, travelers often missed their homes badly.
3. "Thoughts on a Still Night" is very short, with simple wording, but it vividly describes homesickness.

五、回答题

1. 为什么很多中国孩子都会背《静夜思》？
2. 你会背唐诗吗？会背哪几首？
3. 为什么古人旅行在外常会有强烈的思乡之情？
4. 从这首诗里，读者可以看到李白诗的什么特色？

六、讨论题

1. 这首短诗的情景是：一个旅行者在一个秋天的晚上，在月光下思念故乡。这里，旅行、秋天、晚上和月亮构成了思念家乡的四个因素。分析一下这四个因素对思乡所起的作用。
2. 这首诗中写了三种关系：举头与低头、望与思、明月与故乡。谈谈这三种关系中的两个方面之间的关系。
3. 你看到月亮会想家吗？如果你会，谈谈你的经历和原因。如果你不会，谈谈月亮会使你想起什么。

七、专题研究

1. 找一首英文的咏月诗，用中文把它介绍给你的同学，并比较它和中文的咏月诗的相同和不同之处。

7

Jade Steps Resentment
玉阶怨

词汇一

1. 阶, jiē: steps, stairs
2. 怨, yuàn: resentment, grievance
3. 露, lù: dew
4. 侵, qīn: to invade, to erode
5. 罗, luó: silk gauze
6. 下, xià: to lower
7. 水晶, shuǐjīng: crystal
8. 帘, lián: curtain, blinds
9. 玲珑, línglóng: bright and exquisite

玉阶怨

玉阶生白露，夜久侵罗袜。
却下水晶帘，玲珑望秋月。

赏析

  这首诗描写的是一个宫廷妇女在等待皇帝时的情景。古代的皇帝有一个皇后和很多皇妃。皇妃往往很少能见到皇帝，经常在等待中度过日子。

  这个皇妃在宫殿前的白玉台阶上等待皇帝的到来。夜已深，以致露水沾湿了她的罗袜。终于，她失望地走进房间，放下了帘子。可是，怀着一线希望，她透过帘子，望着玲珑的秋月，寄托她的思念。

  这首诗中用了不少晶亮的意象：玉阶、白露、罗袜、水晶帘、玲珑、和秋月，既是宫殿环境的描写，也传达了清冷的感觉。四句诗中一个"怨"字也没有。前两句写秋天的夜景，后两句写女子的动作，但读者能体会到她的等待、失望、哀怨的心情。这是中国诗歌中常用的情景交融的手法。

词汇二

1. **宫廷**, gōngtíng: palace
2. **皇后**, huánghòu: empress
3. **皇妃**, huángfēi: imperial concubine
4. **以致**, yǐzhì: so that, consequently
5. **沾**, zhān: to moisten, to wet
6. **失望**, shīwàng: disappointed
7. **怀**, huái: to cherish, to keep in mind
8. **一线希望**, yíxiàn xīwàng: a ray of hope
9. **透过**, tòuguò: through
10. **寄托**, jìtuō: to place (hope, etc.) on
11. **意象**, yìxiàng: mental images, imagery
12. **传达**, chuándá: to convey, to reveal
13. **清冷**, qīnglěng: chilly and deserted
14. **感觉**, gǎnjué: perception, feeling
15. **哀怨**, āiyuàn: sorrowful and resentful
16. **情景交融**, qíngjǐng jiāoróng: to fuse scene with feeling (in writing)
17. **手法**, shǒufǎ: (artistic) skill, technique

练习

一、选择题

1. 这首诗 _____ 的是一个宫廷妇女在等待皇帝时的情景。

      a. 寄托   **b.** 传达

      c. 探索   **d.** 描写

2. 这些晶亮的意象既是宫殿环境的描写，也传达了清冷的 _____ 。

      a. 感想   **b.** 感觉

      c. 感情   **d.** 感动

3. 这是中国诗歌中常用的情景交融的 _____ 。

      a. 方法   **b.** 办法

      c. 手法   **d.** 做法

二、造句

1. 以致   2. 终于   3. 失望   4. 寄托   5. 传达

6. 感觉   7. 一线希望   8. 手法

三、中译英

1. 玉阶生白露，夜久侵罗袜。

2. 皇妃虽然住在漂亮的皇宫里，但却很孤独，生活得并不快乐。

3. 同样的一个月亮，心情不同的人看着它就会有不同的感觉。

4. 怀着一线希望，她透过帘子，望着玲珑的秋月，寄托她的思念。

四、英译中

1. This poem describes the feeling of a palace lady while she waits for the emperor.

2. Finally, she went into her room with disappointment and pulled down the blinds.

3. The first two lines depict the night scene in autumn, and the last two lines describe the lady's actions.

4. The reader can understand her feelings of disappointment and resentment.

五、回答题

1. 这首诗描写的是一个什么样的人物？
2. 为什么皇妃经常是在等待中度过日子？
3. 你怎么知道夜已经很深了？
4. 她为什么放下帘子后还望着月亮？

六、讨论题

1. 这首诗中每句有一个动词。请找出这四个动词，并说明它们对表达主题所起的作用。
2. 这首《玉阶怨》中一个"怨"字都没用，那位皇妃的怨情是怎么表达出来的？
3.《玉阶怨》和《静夜思》是两首望月诗。比较两首诗中望月的人物、地点，对月光的描写以及由望月引起的思念。

七、作文

1. 题目：《望月》。

8

Gazing into Antiquity at
Su Terrace
苏台览古

词汇一

1. **苏台**, Sūtái: Su Terrace
2. **览**, lǎn: to look at, to see, to view
3. **苑**, yuàn: garden, park
4. **荒**, huāng: desolate
5. **杨柳**, yángliǔ: willow
6. **菱**, líng: water chestnut
7. **不胜**, bùshēng: unbearable, overwhelming
8. **只今**, zhǐjīn: now
9. **惟**, wéi: 只

苏台览古

旧苑荒台杨柳新，菱歌清唱不胜春。
只今惟有西江月，曾照吴王宫里人。

赏析

苏台是春秋时期吴国的一个宫殿，在现在的江苏省苏州市。吴王夫差在那儿跟有名的美人西施一起日夜游玩。

诗人到一个有古迹的地方，常常要写一首诗来抒发对古今变迁的感想。这种诗叫"怀古诗"。

这首诗的题目叫《苏台览古》，前两句写苏台，后两句写览古。第一句写苏台的景观，"旧苑荒台"与"杨柳新"成对比。昔日辉煌的苏台已成陈迹，而自然界的杨柳却依旧充满春意。第二句进一步写眼前的春天景色：台边江上的小船中，姑娘们一边采菱，一边歌唱。第三句突然在空间上来了个飞跃，写到天上的月亮。第四句在时间上横跨历史，追溯到古代。当年吴王与西施欢乐之景，只有西江明月见过。如今明月依旧高悬，而美人不复可见。这是多么深沉的感叹啊！

词汇二

1. **春秋**, Chūnqiū: the Spring and Autumn Period (770–476 BCE)
2. **吴国**, Wúguó: Wu Kingdom
3. **江苏**, Jiāngsū: Jiangsu Province
4. **苏州**, Sūzhōu: a city in Jiangsu Province
5. **夫差**, Fūchāi: King of Wu (d. 473 BCE)
6. **西施**, Xīshī: a beautiful lady in the Spring and Autumn Period
7. **抒发**, shūfā: to express (poetically)
8. **怀古**, huáigǔ: to meditate on the past
9. **景观**, jǐngguān: scene, landscape
10. **对比**, duìbǐ: contrast
11. **昔日**, xīrì: 过去、从前
12. **辉煌**, huīhuáng: splendid and majestic
13. **陈迹**, chénjī: relics, vestiges
14. **依旧**, yījiù: as before, still
15. **采**, cǎi: to pick, to pluck
16. **空间**, kōngjiān: space
17. **飞跃**, fēiyuè: to leap
18. **横跨**, héngkuà: to stretch over or across
19. **追溯**, zhuīsù: to trace back
20. **悬**, xuán: to hang
21. **复**, fù: 再
22. **深沉**, shēnchén: deep, somber
23. **感叹**, gǎntàn: sigh with emotion

练习

一、选择题

1. 苏台是春秋时期吴国的一个宫殿，在现在的江苏省的 _____ 市。
     a. 南京   b. 上海
     c. 苏州   d. 杭州

2. 诗人到一个有古迹的地方，常常要写一首诗来 _____ 对古今变迁的感想。
     a. 抒情   b. 抒发
     c. 发表   d. 表现

3. 第四句在时间上横跨历史，追溯到 _____ 。
     a. 古代   b. 近代
     c. 现代   d. 当代

二、造句

1. 抒发   2. 景观   3. 对比   4. 昔日   5. 辉煌
6. 依旧   7. 深沉   8. 感叹

三、中译英

1. 只今惟有西江月，曾照吴王宫里人。

2. 苏州是春秋时吴国的国都，有很多名胜古迹，也有很多有名的园林。

3. 西施是中国历史上有名的美女，她的故事出现在很多小说和电影里。

4. 古人到一个有历史古迹的地方去游览的时候，常常会产生对古今变迁的感叹。

四、英译中

1. Su Terrace was a palace of the Wu Kingdom. It was in present-day Suzhou in Jiangsu Province.

2. The first line presents the scene of Su Terrace, where the old gardens and desolate terrace contrast with fresh willows.

3. On the small boats in the river, girls are singing while picking water chestnuts.
4. The bright moon witnessed the joyful parties of King of Wu and the famous beauty Xishi.

五、回答题

1. 苏台是哪个时期的宫殿？在现在的什么地方？
2. 台边江上的小船中，姑娘们在做什么？
3. 吴王夫差跟谁在苏台日夜游玩？
4. 从内容上来说，《苏台览古》是一首什么诗？

六、讨论题

1. 对比是常用的修辞手法。请讲一下第一句中的对比的作用。
2. 这首怀古诗表达了诗人什么样的思想感情？

七、专题研究

1. 吴王夫差和西施的故事。
2. 作文：选一个你去过的历史古迹，写一篇"怀古"的文章。

9

To Wang Changling from Afar, on Hearing of His Demotion to Longbiao
闻王昌龄左迁龙标遥有此寄

词汇一

1. **闻**, wén: 听，听到
2. **王昌龄**, Wáng Chānglíng: a Tang poet (ca. 698–ca. 756)
3. **左迁**, zuǒqiān: to be demoted
4. **龙标**, Lóngbiāo: a city in today's Hunan 湖南 Province
5. **遥**, yáo: 远
6. **杨花**, yánghuā: catkin
7. **子规**, zǐguī: cuckoo
8. **啼**, tí: to cry, to crow
9. **闻道**, wéndào: 听说
10. **五溪**, Wǔxī: the collective name for the five streams in the west of Hunan Province

闻王昌龄左迁龙标遥有此寄

杨花落尽子规啼，闻道龙标过五溪。
我寄愁心与明月，随风直到夜郎西。

赏析

　　首句写景，并点明暮春季节。杨花本来就飘散不定，现在都落尽了，更给人一种飘零的感觉。子规鸟，古人描写它的叫声象在说"不如归去"，会引起思念之情。一个视觉，一个听觉，给全诗创造出一种感伤的气氛。

　　第二句中的"龙标"指王昌龄，他被贬为龙标尉。古人常用一个人的官职来代替他的名字。这句说明诗人写诗的原因和忧愁的由来。

　　第三、第四句显示了诗人的丰富的想象力。夜郎在湖南，跟李白后来的流放地同名，但不是一个地方。"夜郎西"指的是龙标。因为两人离得很远，没法见面，诗人就把自己的愁心寄托给明月，让它随风飘去，带给好友。

词汇二

1. **首**, shǒu: head, first
2. **点明**, diǎnmíng: to point out
3. **暮春**, mùchūn: late spring
4. **飘散**, piāosàn: drifting and scattering
5. **飘零**, piāolíng: leaves falling; people leading a wandering life
6. **视觉**, shìjué: visual sense, vision
7. **听觉**, tīngjué: sense of hearing
8. **感伤**, gǎnshāng: sad, sentimental
9. **气氛**, qìfēn: atmosphere
10. **贬**, biǎn: to demote
11. **尉**, wèi: a military officer
12. **官职**, guānzhí: official position
13. **由来**, yóulái: origin
14. **显示**, xiǎnshì: to show, to display

练习

一、选择题

1. 王昌龄被贬为 _____ 尉。
   - a. 龙标
   - b. 五溪
   - c. 夜郎
   - d. 湖南

2. "杨花落尽子规啼"给全诗创造出一种感伤的 _____ 。
   - a. 环境
   - b. 气氛
   - c. 情况
   - d. 情景

3. 杨花本来就 _____ 不定,现在都落尽了。
   - a. 漂泊
   - b. 漂流
   - c. 飘散
   - d. 飘零

4. 诗人把自己的愁心 _____ 给明月,让它随风飘去,带给好友。
   - a. 显示
   - b. 显露
   - c. 抒发
   - d. 寄托

二、造句

1. 点明　　2. 暮春　　3. 感伤　　4. 气氛　　5. 由来
6. 显示

三、中译英

1. 我寄愁心与明月,随风直到夜郎西。
2. 暮春季节,杨花落尽,子规鸟啼,令人感伤。
3. 一首诗往往从写景开始,再引出叙事、议论和抒情。

四、英译中

1. A visual image, coupled with an auditory sense, created a sad atmosphere for the poem.
2. This line tells the reason for writing this poem and the cause of the poet's sorrow.

3. In ancient times, people were often referred to by their official positions instead of their names.

五、回答题

1. 王昌龄被贬到什么地方？去做什么官？
2. 李白写这首诗的时候是什么季节？你怎么知道？
3. 为什么子规鸟的叫声会引起思念之情？
4. 李白是怎么表达他对王昌龄的思念之情的？

六、讨论题

1. 首句写景，但又情景交融，请说明。
2. 这首诗中的月亮跨越了巨大的空间。在《苏台览古》中，月亮跨越了漫长的历史。结合这两首诗，谈谈李白的丰富的想象力。

七、专题研究

1. 介绍王昌龄的诗：《出塞》或《芙蓉楼送辛渐》。

10

Asking the Moon,
with Wine in Hand
把酒问月

词汇一

1. **把**, bǎ: to hold

2. **之**, zhī: him, her, it

3. **临**, lín: to approach, to reach

4. **丹**, dān: 红

5. **阙**, què: palace

6. **辉**, huī: light, brilliance

7. **发**, fā: to emit, to radiate

8. **宵**, xiāo: night

9. **宁**, nìng: 难道

10. **晓**, xiǎo: dawn

11. **没**, mò: to sink, to be submerged, to disappear

12. **兔**, tù: rabbit, hare

13. **捣**, dǎo: to pound with a pestle

14. **嫦娥**, Cháng'é: goddess of the moon, who swallowed elixir stolen from her husband and then flew to the moon

15. **孤**, gū: lone, solitary

16. **栖**, qī: to perch, to dwell, to stay

17. **若**, ruò: 象

18. **皆**, jiē: 都

19. **唯**, wéi: 只

20. **当**, dāng: 应该

21. **尊**, zūn: goblet

把酒问月

青天有月来几时？我今停杯一问之。
人攀明月不可得，月行却与人相随。
皎如飞镜临丹阙，绿烟灭尽清辉发。
但见宵从海上来，宁知晓向云间没？
白兔捣药秋复春，嫦娥孤栖与谁邻？
今人不见古时月，今月曾经照古人。
古人今人若流水，共看明月皆如此。
唯愿当歌对酒时，月光长照金尊里。

赏析

月亮与酒是李白喜爱的两个题材，这首诗把两者结合起来了。

第一联以问句开头："青天有月来几时？"这个问句表面上来看像是醉话，实际上是对宇宙的奥秘的探索。

第二联写人与月的关系。明月高挂天空，使人觉得高不可攀。然而当你行走时，他却会跟随。两句一远一近，显出月亮既无情又有情，写出月亮对人既神秘又可亲的关系。

第三联对月色进行描绘。第四、第五联又是问月，接连提了两个问题。在中国神话中，月亮上有一位叫嫦娥的仙女，还有一只白兔在不停地捣仙药。这里，以仙女为契机，诗人从对宇宙的探索转向对人生的思考。

第六、第七联将人生短暂、明月永存的哲理写得深入浅出，从而引出最后一联。既然人生如梦，不如及时行乐，明白地表达了道家思想。

全诗从停杯问月开始，到月照酒杯结束。月亮与人生对比，哲理与诗情交融。

词汇二

1. **题材**, tícái: subject matter, theme
2. **神秘**, shénmì: mysterious
3. **契机**, qìjī: turning point, juncture
4. **哲理**, zhélǐ: philosophical theory, philosophy
5. **深入浅出**, shēnrù qiǎnchū: to explain the profound in simple terms
6. **从而**, cóng'ér: thus, thereby
7. **引出**, yǐnchū: to draw forth
8. **既然**, jìrán: since, as, now that
9. **不如**, bùrú: it would be better to

练习

一、选择题

1. 月亮与酒是李白喜爱的两个 _____ 。
   - a. 题材
   - b. 题目
   - c. 主题
   - d. 问题

2. 诗人从对宇宙的探索转向对人生的 _____ 。
   - a. 思想
   - b. 思念
   - c. 思考
   - d. 思虑

3. 第六、第七联将人生短暂、明月永存的哲理写得 _____ 。
   - a. 高不可攀
   - b. 深入浅出
   - c. 情景交融
   - d. 源远流长

二、造句

1. 题材   2. 神秘   3. 哲理   4. 深入浅出   5. 从而
6. 引出   7. 既然   8. 不如

三、中译英

1. 青天有月来几时？我今停杯一问之。
2. 人攀明月不可得，月行却与人相随。
3. 今人不见古时月，今月曾经照古人。
4. 既然人生如梦，不如及时行乐。
5. 嫦娥是中国的月亮女神。月饼盒子上常常画着嫦娥。

四、英译中

1. The moon and wine drinking are two favorite themes of Li Bai's.
2. "How long has the moon been in the blue sky?" This question sounds like one from a drunken person, but is in fact an exploration of the mysteries of the universe.
3. The poet turns from exploration of the cosmos to the pondering of human life.
4. The last four lines express the Daoist ideas of life as a dream and making merry in a timely fashion.

五、回答题

1. 这首诗的第一句有哪两层意思?
2. 李白在这首诗中问了哪三个问题?
3. 李白是怎么描写月色的?

六、讨论题

1. 这首诗中的"今人不见古时月, 今月曾经照古人"与
《苏台览古》中的"只今惟有西江月, 曾照吴王宫里人"
意思相近。这两联反映了诗人的什么思想? 请说明。
2. 本书选的五首咏月诗, 写了诗人在月光下不同的行为和
思想。《静夜思》是思乡, 《玉阶怨》是等人, 《苏台览
古》是怀古, 《闻王昌龄左迁龙标遥有此寄》是想念远方
的朋友, 这首《把酒问月》则是探索宇宙、人生的道理。
请讲一下这五首诗中写的不同的环境以及由此而产生的不
同的想法。

七、专题研究

1. 宋代苏轼的词《水调歌头》明显受到李白这首诗的影
响。介绍一下苏轼的这首词。
2. 讲一下嫦娥奔月的神话故事。

11

A Brief Introduction to Mountain-and-Water Poetry
山水诗小序

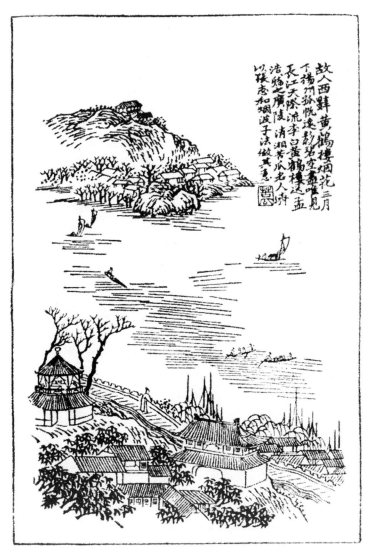

故人西辞黄鹤楼烟花三月
下扬州孤帆远影碧空尽唯见
长江天际流李白黄鹤楼送孟
浩然之广陵 清湘芳氏老人村
以孤志和烟波子法做其意

黄鹤楼送孟浩然

词汇一

1. **体裁**, tǐcái: literary form, genre
2. **秀丽**, xiùlì: beautiful and graceful
3. **壮丽**, zhuànglì: beautiful and majestic
4. **雄伟**, xióngwěi: grand, magnificent
5. **开阔**, kāikuò: broad, wide
6. **活力**, huólì: vigor, vitality
7. **注入**, zhùrù: to pour into, to instill, to infuse
8. **赋予**, fùyǔ: to bestow
9. **瀑布**, pùbù: waterfall
10. **庐山**, Lúshān: Mount Lu, in Jiangxi 江西 Province
11. **奔流**, bēnliú: to flow at great speed; rushing water
12. **姿态**, zītài : posture

小序

　　山水诗是中国古典诗歌中的一种特殊的体裁，描写以山水为主的风景。李白一生漫游大半个中国，写了很多山水诗。

　　李白的山水诗有两个主要特点。一个是风格上的。李白的前人大都描写秀丽的景色，李白的山水诗却以壮丽为主。他笔下的山水大都雄伟开阔，充满活力，给人以力量。另一个特点是李白不但描写山水的外貌，而且描写山水的精神。也就是说，李白将自己的感情注入了山水之中，赋予它们生命。如李白写瀑布的名句："飞流直下三千尺"（《望庐山瀑布》），不但写出了瀑布奔流的姿态，也写出了诗人奔放的性格。山水和诗人完全融合在一起。

练习

一、选择题

1. 山水诗是中国古典诗歌中的一种特殊的 _____ 。
   - **a.** 题材
   - **b.** 体裁
   - **c.** 题目
   - **d.** 体例

2. 李白一生 _____ 大半个中国。
   - **a.** 漫游
   - **b.** 旅游
   - **c.** 游览
   - **d.** 游玩

3. 李白的山水诗以 _____ 为主。
   - **a.** 美丽
   - **b.** 华丽
   - **c.** 秀丽
   - **d.** 壮丽

4. 李白的这句诗写出了诗人 _____ 的性格。
   - **a.** 奔流
   - **b.** 奔腾
   - **c.** 奔放
   - **d.** 奔驰

二、造句

1. 漫游　　2. 秀丽　　3. 壮丽　　　4. 雄伟　　5. 活力

6. 赋予　　7. 奔流　　8. 奔放

三、中译英

1. 李白和杜甫都写了很多山水诗，但他们的风格很不一样。李白的山水诗是写意的，杜甫是写实的。

2. 很多中国人在家中挂一幅山水画，也有人喜欢挂花鸟画。

3. 中国有很多有名的山，如泰山、黄山、庐山、峨眉山等，各有特色。泰山雄伟壮丽，黄山风景秀丽，庐山多峭壁、瀑布，峨眉山是佛教名山。

四、英译中

1. Li Bai traveled through more than half of China and wrote many mountain-and-water poems.

2. Not only do Li Bai's poems describe the appearance of mountains and waters, but they also describe their spirit.

3. Li Bai instills his own feelings into mountains and waters and bestows life on them.

五、回答题

1. 什么是山水诗？

2. 李白的前人大都描写什么样的景色？

3. 李白的山水诗以什么为主？

六、讨论题

1. 李白山水诗有哪两个主要特点？请具体说明。

七、专题研究

1. 李白、杜甫都写了不少山水诗。唐朝的另一位大诗人王维也是有名的山水诗人。介绍一下王维的山水诗。（关键词：王维、山水诗、诗中有画、辋川集）

12

Gazing at
Heavenly Gate Mountain
望天门山

词汇一

1. **天门山**, Tiānmén Shān: mountains in Dangtu County of Anhui Province; the mountains on the banks of the Yangtze River look like the pillars of a gate

2. **断**, duàn: severed, broken

3. **楚江**, Chǔjiāng: referring to this particular portion of the Yangtze River, since Dangtu was in the State of Chu 楚 during the Warring States 战国 period (403–221 BCE)

4. **碧**, bì: blue, emerald green

5. **洄**, huí: to whirl (of water)

望天门山

天门中断楚江开，碧水东流至此回。
两岸青山相对出，孤帆一片日边来。

赏析

公元七二五年夏秋之交，二十四岁的李白初次乘船过天门山，写下了这首诗。

诗题中有一望字，但诗中却没有望字。实际上，又是句句写望，只是望的角度和立足点不同。

首句兼写山水，是远望。在诗人的想象中，奔腾的长江冲断了天门山，有冲决一切阻碍的神奇力量。这种气势是李白诗的一个特色。

次句写水，是近望。江水在受到山岩阻挡时，波涛翻滚回旋。

第三句是船行至天门山之间时诗人左右望，观看两岸层出不穷的山景。人们都有这样的体会：有时坐在车、船上，不觉得车、船在行进，反而觉得周围的景物在移动。第四句又写水，是远望。船驶出天门山后，江面开阔，诗人遥望日边来的风帆。

全诗四句，像一组电影镜头，由远而近，又由近而远。随着诗人的"望"，展现了一幅壮丽的山水画。此诗虽然没直接表达诗人的情绪，但在字里行间，我们能体会到年轻的诗人的愉快心情。他富有青春活力，对前途充满希望。

词汇二

1. **交**, jiāo: juncture, junction
2. **初次**, chūcì: 第一次
3. **角度**, jiǎodù: angle, perspective
4. **立足点**, lìzúdiǎn: foothold, standpoint
5. **兼**, jiān: simultaneously, concurrently
6. **(冲)决**, jué: to breach, to burst
7. **阻碍**, zǔ'ài: obstacle, hindrance
8. **气势**, qìshì: imposing manner, momentum
9. **岩**, yán: rock, cliff
10. **阻挡**, zǔdǎng: to stop, to hinder, to resist
11. **波涛**, bōtāo: great waves, billows
12. **翻滚**, fāngǔn: to roll, to tumble
13. **回旋**, huíxuán: to circle round, to whirl (of water)

14. **层出不穷**, céngchū bùqióng: to emerge one after another

15. **反而**, fǎn'ér: on the contrary, instead

16. **驶**, shǐ: to sail, to drive

17. **字里行间**, zìlǐ hángjiān: between the lines

18. **情绪**, qíngxù: feeling, mood, sentiment

19. **富有**, fùyǒu: rich in, full of

练习

一、选择题

1. 奔腾的长江冲断了天门山，有冲决一切 _____ 的神奇力量。
   - **a.** 阻挡
   - **b.** 阻止
   - **c.** 阻碍
   - **d.** 阻隔

2. 这种 _____ 是李白诗的一个特色。
   - **a.** 气势
   - **b.** 气力
   - **c.** 气氛
   - **d.** 气色

3. 有时坐在车、船上，不觉得车、船在行进， _____ 觉得周围的景物在移动。
   - **a.** 总是
   - **b.** 还是
   - **c.** 反而
   - **d.** 而且

4. 全诗四句，像一 _____ 电影镜头。
   - **a.** 群
   - **b.** 批
   - **c.** 排
   - **d.** 组

二、造句

1. 初次   2. 角度   3. 兼   4. 阻碍   5. 气势

6. 阻挡   7. 波涛   8. 反而   9. 字里行间   10. 富有

三、中译英

1. 两岸青山相对出，孤帆一片日边来。

2. 李白这首山水诗生动地描写了长江和天门山的风景。根据这首诗的诗意，很容易画一幅山水画：有奔腾的长江、奇特的天门山、远处的一片孤帆和一轮落日。

四、英译中

1. In the poet's imagination, the surging Yangtze River breached the Heavenly Gate Mountains.
2. When the boat moved in between the Heavenly Gate Mountains, the poet looked left and right, observing the view of the mountains.
3. We can feel the poet's happy mood between the lines.

五、回答题

1. 这首诗是在哪一年写的？当时李白几岁？
2. 诗题中有一"望"字，在诗中有没有用"望"字？
3. 为什么李白会有"两岸青山相对出"的感觉？
4. 从这首诗里，我们能体会到年轻诗人的什么样的心情？

六、讨论题

1. 山水诗中常常一句写山、一句写水。请分析这首诗中四句诗描写山水的分工。
2. 李白在这首诗中是怎么望天门山的？请逐句分析。
3. 这首诗四句都是写景,并无直接的抒情，但读者能在字里行间体会到诗人的感情。请说明这首诗是怎么做到情景交融的。

七、作文

1. 根据自己的经历，写一篇观看山景的作文。

13

Gazing at a Waterfall
on Mount Lu
望庐山瀑布

词汇一

1. **香炉**, Xiānglú: 香炉峰, Incense Burner Peak on Mount Lu *庐山*
2. **紫**, zǐ: purple
3. **川**, chuān: river
4. **银河**, Yínhé: the Milky Way
5. **九天**, jiǔtiān: the Ninth Heaven, the highest level of Heaven

望庐山瀑布

日照香炉生紫烟，遥看瀑布挂前川。
飞流直下三千尺，疑是银河落九天。

赏析

　　瀑布是山和水的结合，也是李白喜爱描写的对象。这首诗第一句写香炉峰的美景："紫烟"是瀑布的水汽在阳光照耀下所形成的彩色云雾。第二句写瀑布的静态：远远望去，它好像一条白练高高地挂在山上。第三句写瀑布的气势磅礴的动态。一静一动，画出了庐山瀑布壮丽的奇景。最后一句显示了诗人奇特的想象力。

　　诗中后三句用了不同的艺术手法描写瀑布："遥看瀑布挂前川"是比喻，"飞流直下三千尺"是夸张，"疑是银河落九天"是想象。用在一起，创造了这首千古传诵的瀑布诗。

词汇二

1. **水汽**, shuǐqì: vapor, steam
2. **照耀**, zhàoyào: to shine on
3. **形成**, xíngchéng: to take shape, to form
4. **静态**, jìngtài: static state
5. **练**, liàn: white silk
6. **挂**, guà: to hang
7. **磅礴**, pángbó: extensive, majestic
8. **动态**, dòngtài: dynamic state

练习

一、选择题

1. 瀑布是山和水的 _____ 。
    a. 配合   b. 结合
    c. 联合   d. 符合

2. "飞流直下三千尺" 是 _____ 。
    a. 想象   b. 比喻
    c. 夸张   d. 象征

3. 第三句写瀑布的 _____ 的动态。
    a. 气势磅礴   b. 千古传颂
    c. 层出不穷   d. 雄伟开阔

4. 最后一句显示了诗人 _____ 的想象力。
    a. 壮丽   b. 奇特
    c. 奔放   d. 富有

二、造句

1. 照耀   2. 形成   3. 挂   4. 气势磅礴   5. 动态

三、中译英

1. 飞流直下三千尺，疑是银河落九天。
2. 中国贵州省的黄果树瀑布和在美国与加拿大边境上的尼亚加拉瀑布都是有名的大瀑布。
3. 庐山不但风景秀丽，而且气候宜人，所以也是个休养胜地。

四、英译中

1. Waterfalls were Li Bai's favorite subject.
2. Watching from afar, the waterfall looked like a piece of white cloth hanging on the high mountain.
3. These three lines of waterfall description use different artistic devices.

五、回答题

1. 第一句里说的 "紫烟" 是什么?
2. 远远望去,庐山瀑布像什么?
3. 第二、第三句对瀑布的描写有什么不同?

六、讨论题

1. 这首诗里用了比喻、夸张和想象,请分别举例说明。

七、作文

1. 比喻、夸张和想象是文学创作中常用的艺术手法。写一篇自己命题的山水游记短文,文中要用这三种手法分别形容一条奔腾的大河和一座高峻的大山。

14

Seeing Meng Haoran Off to Guangling at the Yellow Crane Tower

黄鹤楼送孟浩然之广陵

词汇一

1. **黄鹤楼**, Huánghèlóu: the Yellow Crane Tower, in today's Wuhan 武汉 City of Hubei 湖北 Province
2. **孟浩然**, Mèng Hàorán: Tang poet (689–ca. 740)
3. **之**, zhī: 去、到
4. **广陵**, Guǎnglíng: today's Yangzhou 扬州, in Jiangsu Province
5. **故人**, gùrén: 老朋友
6. **辞**, cí: 告别
7. **烟花**, yānhuā: a description of the spring scene with flowers blooming
8. **下**, xià: to go downstream
9. **天际**, tiānjì: 天边

黄鹤楼送孟浩然之广陵

故人西辞黄鹤楼，烟花三月下扬州。
孤帆远影碧空尽，唯见长江天际流。

赏析

　　首句交代两位朋友分别的地点：在长江边上，著名的黄鹤楼边。黄鹤楼在武汉，在扬州的西边，所以说"西辞"。第二句讲明季节，正是垂柳如烟，繁花似锦的春天。这里说的"三月"是中国农历，差不多是西方日历的四月。扬州是当时东南地区繁华的都会。虽然两人要分手了，但美好的季节、地点和旅行目的地，都冲淡了离别之愁。

　　第三、第四句写孟浩然登舟而去，李白在江边目送。一片白帆离诗人越来越远，只能看到很小的影子，最后消失在碧空的尽头。此时，诗人还在远望，可是望到的只有长江在天边流。这两句写的是诗人眼中江景，但读者却能看到在黄鹤楼边久久不肯离开的诗人，并体会到他的惜别之情。

词汇二

1. **交代**, jiāodài: to explain, to make clear
2. **垂柳**, chuíliǔ: weeping willow
3. **垂**, chuí: to droop
4. **繁**, fán: numerous, abundant
5. **锦**, jǐn: brocade
6. **农历**, nónglì: Chinese lunar calendar
7. **繁华**, fánhuá: flourishing
8. **都会**, dūhuì: metropolis
9. **冲淡**, chōngdàn: to dilute, to weaken
10. **登**, dēng: to ascend, to board
11. **舟**, zhōu: 船
12. **目送**, mùsòng: to follow with the eyes
13. **惜别**, xībié: to be reluctant to part with

练习

一、选择题

1. 黄鹤楼在 _____ 。
   - a. 扬州
   - b. 武汉
   - c. 成都
   - d. 西安

2. 扬州在 _____ 省。
   - a. 湖北
   - b. 四川
   - c. 陕西
   - d. 江苏

3. 美好的季节、地点和旅行目的地，都 _____ 了离别之愁。
   - a. 冲淡
   - b. 加深
   - c. 延长
   - d. 阻挡

4. 读者能体会到诗人的 _____ 之情。
   - a. 离别
   - b. 告别
   - c. 惜别
   - d. 分别

二、造句

1. 交代　　2. 农历　　3. 繁华　　4. 都会　　5. 冲淡
6. 登　　　7. 惜别

三、中译英

1. 孤帆远影碧空尽，唯见长江天际流。
2. 暮春三月，垂柳如烟，繁花似锦。
3. 孟浩然是唐朝著名的山水诗人，和王维并称"王孟"。
4. 中国的农历也叫阴历。农历的季节很容易算：一、二、三月是春天，四、五、六月是夏天，七、八、九月是秋天，十、十一、十二月是冬天。

四、英译中

1. Yangzhou was a flourishing metropolis of southeast China at that time.

2. Meng Haoran boarded the boat and left while Li Bai was seeing him off at the riverside.

3. The white sail became smaller and smaller, and finally disappeared into the horizon of the blue sky.

五、回答题

1. 为什么李白说孟浩然 是"西辞黄鹤楼"？
2. "烟花三月"是什么意思？
3. 中国农历上的"三月"大概是西方日历上的几月？
4. 李白是怎样表达他对孟浩然的惜别之情的？

六、讨论题

1. 根据这首诗的诗意画一幅画，并把这首诗写在画上，然后讲一下你的这幅诗意画。
2. 查一查中国地图，简单介绍一下从黄鹤楼到扬州的旅程。
3. 孟浩然和王昌龄都是唐朝的著名诗人，也都是李白的好朋友。比较这首诗和《闻王昌龄左迁龙标遥有此寄》中李白关于友谊的描写：环境、季节、心情和表现手法有哪些相同和不同之处。

七、专题研究

1. 诗人孟浩然和他的诗《春晓》。

15

Morning Departure from Baidi City

早发白帝城

词汇一

1. **早**, zǎo: 早上
2. **发**, fā: 出发
3. **朝**, zhāo: 早上
4. **江陵**, Jiānglíng: a city in Hubei Province
5. **还**, huán: 返回
6. **猿**, yuán: gibbon
7. **重**, chóng: layer

早发白帝城

朝辞白帝彩云间，千里江陵一日还。
两岸猿声啼不住，轻舟已过万重山。

赏析

　　如本书《李白小传》中所说，李白因为参加永王的军队被判流放夜郎。公元七五九年三月，李白在途经白帝城时遇到大赦。白帝城是一座古城，在四川省，位于长江三峡的边上。这首诗就是李白乘船东归时写的。

　　首句点明出发的时间、地点。"彩云间"这个短语有多种作用。它既描绘了早晨的美景，又说明了白帝城地势之高，为下句船速之快伏笔。同时，它也表达了诗人的好心情。同样的景色，在不同的人的眼中，会有不同的感受。李白说他在"彩云间"出发，流露出他的喜悦和兴奋之情。

　　第二句写舟行速度之快。一个"还"字，表达了遇赦放还的欢快感。"一日还"当然是夸张，也说明诗人的迫切心情。第三句说诗人在船上听猿声，引出第四句"轻舟已过万重山"。"轻舟"这个词也有双重意义。表面上，说明水流之急，觉得船轻其实是因为船开得快。可是更重要的，船的轻快也与诗人心情的轻快相呼应。

词汇二

1. **途经**, tújīng: 路过，经过
2. **三峡**, Sānxiá: The Three Gorges (of the Yangtze River)
3. **短语**, duǎnyǔ: phrase
4. **地势**, dìshì: topography, terrain
5. **伏笔**, fúbǐ: foreshadowing (in writing)
6. **感受**, gǎnshòu: feelings (evoked by something), reflections, perceptions
7. **流露**, liúlù: to reveal, to show unintentionally
8. **迫切**, pòqiè: urgent
9. **其实**, qíshí: actually
10. **轻快**, qīngkuài: brisk, lively, light-hearted
11. **呼应**, hūyìng: to echo each other, to work in concert with

练习

一、选择题

1. "彩云间" 这个 _____ 有多种作用。

      a. 词语   b. 成语

      c. 短语   d. 话语

2. "彩云间" 说明白帝城 _____ 之高。

      a. 地理   b. 地方

      c. 地势   d. 地形

3. 李白说他在 "彩云间" 出发，_____ 出他的喜悦和兴奋之情。

      a. 说明   b. 显示

      c. 流放   d. 流露

4. 船的轻快也与诗人心情的轻快相 _____ 。

      a. 联系   b. 感受

      c. 呼应   d. 答应

二、造句

1. 地势   2. 感受   3. 流露   4. 迫切   5. 其实

6. 轻快   7. 呼应

三、中译英

1. 两岸猿声啼不住，轻舟已过万重山。

2. 三峡大坝高七十米，长两千多米，是世界上最大的水坝。

3. 白帝城一面靠山，三面环水，是三峡旅游线上有名的景点。

4. 诗人觉得船轻其实是因为船开得快，也因为他的心情很轻快。

四、英译中

1. Li Bai received amnesty in Baidi City, Sichuan, on the way to being exiled.

2. This phrase describes the beautiful scene in the morning, and also expresses the poet's good mood.
3. The same scene is often perceived differently by different people.

五、回答题

1. 李白遇赦东归，是在什么时间、从哪里出发的？
2. 你怎么知道白帝城地势很高？
3. 你怎么知道船开得很快？

六、讨论题

1. 举两个例子说明夸张在这首诗中对船速的描写和诗人心情的表达所起的作用。
2. 心情不同的人对同样的景物会有不同的感受，举一个诗中的例子来说明。

七、专题研究

1. 介绍长江三峡的风景、航运和大坝工程。

16

Passing by Jingmen Mountain
渡荆门

词汇一

1. **渡**, dù: to cross (a river, the sea, etc.)
2. **荆门**, Jīngmén: a mountain in Hubei Province
3. **从**, cóng: to follow, to join
4. **楚国**, Chǔguó: a state in the Spring and Autumn Period and the Warring States Period, which is roughly equivalent to today's Hunan and Hubei Provinces
5. **野**, yě: field
6. **结**, jié: to form, to congeal
7. **海楼**, hǎilóu: mirage
8. **仍**, réng: still, yet
9. **怜**, lián: *爱*

渡荆门

渡远荆门外，来从楚国游。
山随平野尽，江入大荒流。
月下飞天镜，云生结海楼。
仍怜故乡水，万里送行舟。

赏析

　　公元七二四年秋，二十三岁的李白离开家乡，"辞亲远游"。他在长江中乘船东下，船到荆门山时，写了这首诗。

　　过了荆门山，意味着离开四川，进入古代称为楚国的地方。首联点明他远游来到荆门，表达了青年诗人进入新天地时的喜悦心情。颔联写舟过荆门山以后，地势平坦的景色。颈联写江行夜景。"月下飞天镜"中的"下"字是个动词。因为视野开阔，远处天边的月亮显得位置很低。在尾联中，诗人面对从故乡流下来的滔滔江水，流露出对故乡的依恋之情。诗人没直说自己思念故乡，却说故乡水为他送行，既是一种拟人的手法，又是一种巧妙的构思。

词汇二

1. **意味**, yìwèi: to mean, to signify, to imply
2. **首联**, shǒulián: 律诗的第一联
3. **颔联**, hànlián: 律诗的第二联
4. **颔**, hàn: the chin, the jaws
5. **平坦**, píngtǎn: (of land, etc.) level, even, smooth
6. **颈联**, jǐnglián: 律诗的第三联
7. **颈**, jǐng: neck
8. **视野**, shìyě: field of vision
9. **位置**, wèizhi: place, position
10. **尾联**, wěilián: 律诗的第四联
11. **尾**, wěi: tail
12. **滔滔**, tāotāo: torrential, surging
13. **依恋**, yīliàn: to be reluctant to leave, to continue to long for
14. **拟人**, nǐrén: personification
15. **巧妙**, qiǎomiào: ingenious, clever
16. **构思**, gòusī: conception, idea, design (of a literary work)

练习

一、选择题

1. 荆门山在 _____ 省。
   - **a.** 四川
   - **b.** 湖北
   - **c.** 江苏
   - **d.** 陕西
2. _____ 写江行夜景。
   - **a.** 首联
   - **b.** 颔联
   - **c.** 颈联
   - **d.** 尾联
3. 因为视野 _____ ，远处天边的月亮显得位置很低。
   - **a.** 开放
   - **b.** 平坦
   - **c.** 辽阔
   - **d.** 开阔
4. 诗人面对从故乡流下来的滔滔江水，流露出对故乡的 _____ 之情。
   - **a.** 依靠
   - **b.** 依恋
   - **c.** 依照
   - **d.** 依旧

二、造句

1. 意味　　2. 平坦　　3. 视野　　4. 依恋　　5. 巧妙
6. 构思

三、中译英

1. 山随平野尽，江入大荒流。
2. 月下飞天镜，云生结海楼。
3. 这是一首五言律诗。李白写诗自由、奔放，所以律诗写得不多。
4. 从这首律诗中，我们可以看到对仗、押韵、声调等规律的具体应用。

四、英译中

1. Passing by Jingmen Mountain means leaving Sichuan and entering the region that was called the State of Chu in ancient times.

2. The first couplet expresses the young poet's happy mood when he enters the new world.

3. Because of the broad field of vision, the moon at the far end of the sky looks to be in a very low position.

五、回答题

1. 在长江中乘船，离开四川省后，就进入哪个省？
2. 湖北、湖南的地方，在春秋战国时代叫什么？
3. 船过荆门山以后，地势怎么样？
4. "月下飞天镜"中的"下"字是个什么词？
5. 为什么月亮会"下来"？

六、讨论题

1. 李白在这首诗中是怎么表达他对故乡的依恋之情的？
2. 《早发白帝城》、《渡荆门送别》和《黄鹤楼送孟浩然之广陵》都是写舟行长江的景色。比较这三首诗中对长江不同段落、不同季节及不同时间的景色描写。
3. 这是一首五言律诗，中间两联是对仗。请具体说明字句是怎么相对的。

七、专题研究

1. 研究对仗的规律并练习对仗：两人为一组，一人出上句，一人对下句。从一字句发展到五字句。

17

A Brief Introduction to
Wine Drinking Poetry
饮酒诗小序

青莲醉酒

词汇一

1. 斗, dǒu: goblet, drinking vessel
2. 天子, tiānzǐ: Son of Heaven, the emperor
3. 呼, hū: to call
4. 臣, chén: a subject under an emperor, a term for "I" used by officials when addressing the emperor
5. 肖像, xiāoxiàng: portrait
6. 畅, chàng: free-flowing and unimpeded
7. 刺激, cìjī: to stimulate
8. 本质, běnzhì: essence, nature
9. 凭借, píngjiè: to rely on, to depend on
10. 激情, jīqíng: passion, enthusiasm
11. 酒意, jiǔyì: tipsy feeling
12. 今朝, jīnzhāo: 今天
13. 借酒浇愁, jièjiǔ jiāochóu: to wash away one's worries with wine
14. 浇, jiāo: to pour, to sprinkle, to irrigate
15. 醉乡, zuìxiāng: realm of drunkenness
16. 仅, jǐn: 只

小序

　　杜甫曾经这样写他的好友李白："李白一斗诗百篇，长安市上酒家眠。天子呼来不上船，自称臣是酒中仙"（《饮中八仙歌》）。这四句诗就像一幅李白的肖像画，描绘了他"诗仙"加"酒仙"的形象。

　　为什么李白能"一斗诗百篇"？为什么李白在醉酒时诗思最畅？在酒的刺激下，诗人往往精神高度兴奋，想象力变得非常活跃。而诗的本质，正是凭借激情和想象的艺术创造。李白的饮酒诗内容丰富：有的带着酒意，批评权贵；有的表现"今朝有酒今朝醉"的及时行乐思想；有的借酒浇愁，追求醉乡的自由。

　　李白诗中写到酒的占总数百分之三十以上。这里我们仅选读四首。

练习

一、选择题

1. 这首诗描绘了李白"诗仙"加"酒仙"的 _____ 。
    a. 形状   **b.** 形象
    c. 形式   **d.** 形势
2. 在酒的刺激下，诗人往往精神高度 _____ 。
    a. 高兴   **b.** 快乐
    c. 兴奋   **d.** 冷静
3. 诗人的想象力非常 _____ 。
    a. 活跃   **b.** 兴奋
    c. 快活   **d.** 灵活

二、造句

1. 刺激   2. 本质   3. 凭借   4. 激情   5. 酒意
6. 仅

三、中译英

1. 李白一斗诗百篇，长安市上酒家眠。
2. 中国古代的诗人大都喜欢喝酒，李白"诗仙"加"酒仙"的形象最生动地体现了这个特点。
3. 民间传说李白在船上喝醉了，要去捉水中的月亮，结果溺死了。虽然这只是传说，但提到了李白诗中写得最多的两件事：饮酒和赏月。

四、英译中

1. This poem is like a portrait of Li Bai, depicting images of him as the "Muse of Poetry" and the "Immortal of Wine."
2. Under wine's influence, poets often get excited and their imaginations become very active.
3. The essence of poetry is artistic creation based on passion and imagination.

五、回答题

1. "李白一斗诗百篇"这个诗句中用了一个什么艺术手法?

2. 李白自称什么?

3. 李白大约写了多少饮酒诗?

六、讨论题

1. 从本课引的杜甫的诗中,我们可以看出李白是怎样的一个人?

2. 为什么李白能"一斗诗百篇"?

3. 李白的饮酒诗中写到了哪些内容?

七、专题研究

1. 李白不但写了很多饮酒诗,还写过一篇很有名的关于饮酒的短文,叫《春夜宴桃李园序》。请介绍一下这篇文章中描写的宴饮场面和表现的哲学思想。

18

Written in an Alien Land
客中作

词汇一

1. **客**, kè: to live or stay in a strange land
2. **兰陵**, Lánlíng: a city in today's Shandong 山东 Province, known for its wine making
3. **郁金香**, yùjīnxiāng: tulip
4. **盛**, chéng: to fill
5. **琥珀**, hǔpò: amber
6. **但使**, dànshǐ: 只要
7. **他乡**, tāxiāng: strange land, land away from home

客中作

兰陵美酒郁金香，玉碗盛来琥珀光。
但使主人能醉客，不知何处是他乡。

赏析

    他乡作客之悲是古代诗歌创作中一个很普遍的主题。这首诗虽题为《客中作》，表达的却是作者的另一种感受。

    首句写酒的香味。著名的兰陵美酒，是用郁金香浸泡加工的，因此酒香扑鼻。次句写酒的颜色。盛在晶莹的玉碗里，看起来像琥珀般的光艳。诗人面对美酒，愉快兴奋之情自可想见了。

    第三句写主人的热情，第四句写诗人的感受。诗人并非没有意识到是在他乡，当然也并非不想念故乡，但是这些都在兰陵美酒面前被冲淡了。一种乐于在客中、乐于在朋友面前尽情欢醉的情绪支配了他，以至乐而不觉其为他乡。这正是这首诗不同于一般客居他乡之作的地方，也表现了李白豪放的性格。

词汇二

1. **悲**, bēi: sad, sorrowful
2. **浸泡**, jìnpào: to soak, to immerse
3. **加工**, jiāgōng: to process
4. **扑鼻**, pūbí: to come suddenly to one's nostrils (as a strong smell)
5. **光艳**, guāngyàn: bright and colorful
6. **并非**, bìngfēi: by no means
7. **意识**, yìshí: to be aware of, to realize
8. **乐于**, lèyú: to be happy to, to take delight in
9. **尽情**, jìnqíng: to one's heart's content
10. **支配**, zhīpèi: to control, to dominate
11. **以至**, yǐzhì: to such an extent as to

12. **其**, qí: 他 (她、它)，他的 (她的、它的)
13. **豪放**, háofàng: vigorous and unrestrained

练习

一、选择题

1. 这首诗虽题为《客中作》，表达的却是作者的另一种
_____ 。

        a. 感情   b. 感受

        c. 感想   d. 感觉

2. 一种乐于在朋友面前尽情欢醉的 _____ 支配了他。

        a. 想法   b. 思想

        c. 情绪   d. 情感

3. 这首诗表现了李白 _____ 的性格。

        a. 快乐   b. 乐观

        c. 开放   d. 豪放

二、造句

1. 并非   2. 意识   3. 乐于   4. 尽情   5. 支配

6. 以至   7. 其

三、中译英

1. 但使主人能醉客，不知何处是他乡。

2. 李白一生在全国各地漫游，酒就是他的一个好伴侣。

3. 从《静夜思》中我们知道李白也是思念故乡的，喝酒只是他用来暂时忘却这种思念的一个法子罢了。

四、英译中

1. The sorrow of sojourning in an alien land is a common theme of ancient poetry.
2. The poet was by no means unaware of being in an alien land, and was also missing his hometown, but all of these faded in front of the fine wine of Lanling.
3. This is precisely the difference between this poem and most others about sojourning in an alien land.

五、回答题

1. 这首诗的首句写什么？次句写什么？
2. 兰陵美酒是用什么浸泡加工的？
3. 兰陵美酒盛在什么碗里？
4. 兰陵美酒看起来像什么一样光艳？
5. 这首诗表现了李白的什么性格？

六、讨论题

1. 人们常从"色、香、味"三方面来评价食物和饮料。
请根据这首诗，从这三个方面来介绍一下兰陵美酒。
2. 兰陵美酒对客居他乡的李白起了什么作用？
3. 这首诗跟一般的客居他乡之作有什么不同？

七、专题研究

1. 除了兰陵酒以外，中国还有哪些有名的美酒？请介绍
一下。（关键词：茅台、汾酒、竹叶青、五粮液、青岛
啤酒）

19

Drinking Alone
Under the Moon
月下独酌

词汇一

1. 酌, zhuó: to pour out wine, to drink
2. 壶, hú: pot, kettle
3. 既, jì: already, since, as
4. 解, jiě: 懂
5. 徒, tú: merely, in vain
6. 将, jiāng: 与、共
7. 须, xū: must
8. 及, jí: while, just at the moment of
9. 徘徊, páihuái: to pace back and forth, to hesitate
10. 零乱, língluàn: helter-skelter
11. 交欢, jiāohuān: to get along with each other happily
12. 期, qī: to expect, to await, to look forward to
13. 邈, miǎo: 远
14. 云汉, yúnhàn: the Milky Way

月下独酌

花间一壶酒，独酌无相亲。
举杯邀明月，对影成三人。
月既不解饮，影徒随我身。
暂伴月将影，行乐须及春。
我歌月徘徊，我舞影零乱。
醒时同交欢，醉后各分散。
永结无情游，相期邈云汉。

赏析

这首诗既是饮酒诗，也是咏月诗。诗题《月下独酌》包含了三个因素："月下"是环境，"酌"是动作，"独"是方式，更是心情。其中，"独"是贯穿全诗的关键词。

首联直接进入主题。花间月下本是与朋友一起饮酒的好时光，这里却反衬出"独酌无相亲"的冷清。

第二联中，诗人为了摆脱孤独，忽发奇想，邀请天上的明月、地上的身影，跟自己作伴，诗人也因此而"不独"。可是月亮和影子毕竟不会饮酒，所以第三联中，诗人又感到孤独了。

在第四联中，诗人决定和月亮、影子暂时作伴，及时行乐。在第五联中，诗人既歌且舞，在醉中觉得月亮和影子都和他呼应、交流了。这下又不独了。

最后两联表现了李白豁达的人生态度：他与月亮、影子的关系是可分可合，既长久又无情。

词汇二

1. **既是**…**也是**…, jìshì… yěshì…: to be both... and... (to be two things at the same time)
2. **包含**, bāohán: to contain, to include
3. **因素**, yīnsù: factor, element
4. **动作**, dòngzuò: action, movement
5. **贯穿**, guànchuān: to run through, to penetrate
6. **关键**, guānjiàn: key, crux
7. **反衬**, fǎnchèn: to set off by contrast, to serve as a foil to
8. **冷清**, lěngqīng: cold and deserted
9. **摆脱**, bǎituō: to shake off, to break away from
10. **孤独**, gūdú: lonely, solitary
11. **伴**, bàn: companion, partner
12. **毕竟**, bìjìng: after all
13. **既**…**且**…, jì... qiě...: 又…又…
14. **交流**, jiāoliú: to communicate, to exchange
15. **豁达**, huòdá: open-minded, carefree
16. **既**…**又**…, jì... yòu...: both... and... (two characteristics at the same time)

练习

一、选择题

1. 诗题《月下独酌》包含了三个 _____ 。
   - a. 题材
   - b. 主题
   - c. 因素
   - d. 关键

2. 诗题《月下独酌》中的 "酌" 说明 _____ 。
   - a. 环境
   - b. 动作
   - c. 方式
   - d. 心情

3. 诗人为了 _____ 孤独，邀请明月和影子跟自己作伴。
   - a. 摆脱
   - b. 支配
   - c. 阻挡
   - d. 冲淡

4. 诗人在花间月下饮酒，_____ 行乐。
   - a. 暂时
   - b. 及时
   - c. 当时
   - d. 临时

二、造句

1. 包含　　2. 因素　　3. 贯穿　　4. 关键　　5. 透
6. 冷清　　7. 摆脱　　8. 孤独　　9. 毕竟　　10. 交流

三、中译英

1. 花间一壶酒，独酌无相亲。举杯邀明月，对影成三人。
2. 酒和月亮是李白的好朋友。靠着它们，李白才暂时摆脱了孤独寂寞的感觉。
3. 在醉乡中，诗人与大自然融为一体，达到精神自由的境界。

四、英译中

1. The poem's title, "Drinking Alone Under the Moon," includes three elements.
2. In order to free himself from loneliness, the poet invited the moon and his shadow to be his companions.

3. Being drunk, he feels that the moon and his shadow are both communicating with him.

五、回答题

1. 诗题《月下独酌》包含了哪三个因素？
2. 哪个字是贯穿全诗的关键词？
3. 为什么诗人要邀请明月和影子跟自己作伴？

六、讨论题

1. 这首诗充分体现了李白丰富的想象力，请具体说明。
2. 这首诗构思很巧妙，在"独"与"不独"之间进展。请具体分析。
3. 这首诗中"月既不解饮"一句中的"既"字在白话文中也经常使用。讨论《赏析》中"既是…也是"、"既…且"、"既…又"的不同用法，并用这三个句型各造一个句子。
4. 这首《月下独酌》和《把酒问月》都是咏月诗兼饮酒诗。比较这两首诗的写作方法及诗中表现的人生态度。

七、作文

1. 写一篇关于月亮的作文。自行命题。文中要运用丰富的想象。

20

Descending from Zhongnan Mountain, Stopping Overnight and Drinking with Hermit Husi

下终南山过斛斯山人宿置酒

词汇一

1. **终南山**, Zhōngnán Shān: a mountain to the south of Chang'an, where many recluses lived during the Tang
2. **过**, guò: 经过
3. **斛斯**, Húsī: 复姓 (两个字的姓)
4. **山人**, shānrén: hermit, recluse
5. **置**, zhì: to set
6. **暮**, mù: dusk, evening, sunset
7. **顾**, gù: 回头看
8. **径**, jìng: 小路
9. **苍**, cāng: dark green
10. **横**, héng: to permeate
11. **翠微**, cuìwēi: green mountain side
12. **携**, xié: to hold somebody by the hand
13. **田家**, tiánjiā: farmer's family
14. **童稚**, tóngzhì: children
15. **荆扉**, jīngfēi: door of brushwood—poor household
16. **幽**, yōu: deep and secluded
17. **萝**, luó: a kind of creeping plant
18. **拂**, fú: to whisk
19. **憩**, qì: rest
20. **聊**, liáo: tentatively, lightly
21. **挥**, huī: to wave, to wield
22. **河**, hé: 银河 (the Milky Way)
23. **稀**, xī: scarce, sparse
24. **君**, jūn: you (used in addressing a male in formal speech)
25. **陶然**, táorán: happy and carefree
26. **机**, jī: 机会 (opportunity), 机心 (scheming mind)

下终南山过斛斯山人宿置酒

暮从碧山下，山月随人归。
却顾所来径，苍苍横翠微。
相携及田家，童稚开荆扉。
绿竹入幽径，青萝拂行衣。
欢言得所憩，美酒聊共挥。
长歌吟松风，曲尽河星稀。
我醉君复乐，陶然共忘机。

赏析

　　这首诗以在田家饮酒为题材。前四句写"下终南山",为第一部分。后十句写"过斛斯山人宿置酒",为第二部分。每一部分中的层次也很分明。

　　李白到了田家后,先是进门,"童稚开荆扉"。然后经过一条幽径,绿竹夹路,青萝拂衣。最后是住宿和饮酒,一个"挥"字写出了李白开怀畅饮的神情。酒醉情浓,放声高歌,直至凌晨。

　　尾联上句"我醉君复乐"用了古文中"互文见义"的修辞手法,就是说要把一个句子中的两个部分放在一起,互相参照,才能得到完整的理解。所以这个句子不是简单地说李白醉了,斛斯山人很快乐,而是说两人都既醉且乐。末句是抒情,说两人都很愉快,达到心境的平和淡泊。

词汇二

1. **层次**, céngcì: level
2. **分明**, fēnmíng: clear, distinct
3. **夹**, jiā: to press from both sides
4. **开怀畅饮**, kāihuái chàngyǐn: to drink to one's heart's content
5. **怀**, huái: 胸怀, bosom, mind
6. **神情**, shénqíng: expression
7. **浓**, nóng: dense, thick, great, strong
8. **凌晨**, língchéng: wee hours of the morning
9. **修辞**, xiūcí: rhetoric
10. **参照**, cānzhào: to consult, to refer to
11. **心境**, xīnjìng: state of mind, mood
12. **平和**, pínghé: peaceful, gentle
13. **淡泊**, dànbó: to lead a tranquil life without worldly desires

练习

一、选择题

1. 一个 "挥" 字写出了李白开怀畅饮的 _____ 。
  a. 心情   b. 感情
  c. 神情   d. 友情

2. "互文见义" 是说要把一个句子中的两个部分放在一起，互相 _____ ，才能得到完整的理解。
  a. 参照   b. 参考
  c. 参加   d. 参与

3. 这首诗的结尾是 _____ 。
  a. 叙事   b. 写景
  c. 议论   d. 抒情

4. 两人都很快乐，达到 _____ 的平和淡泊。
  a. 心里   b. 心理
  c. 心地   d. 心境

二、造句

1. 层次 2. 浓 3. 凌晨 4. 心境 5. 平和
6. 淡泊

三、中译英

1. 暮从碧山下，山月随人归。
2. 相携及田家，童稚开荆扉。
3. 李白到了田家后，经过一条幽径，绿竹夹路，青萝拂衣。

四、英译中

1. This poem is about drinking in a farmer's house.
2. They drank until they were drunk and recited poems loudly until dawn.
3. The last couplet says that both of them were very happy and reached a peaceful state of mind.

五、回答题

1. 这首诗可分成哪两个部分？
2. 第二部分中有哪些层次？
3. 李白和斛斯山人在饮酒后达到什么样的心境？

六、讨论题

1. 请描写一下斛斯山人家的环境。
2. 这首诗写的是两人对酌。请把这首诗与《月下独酌》做一个比较。在饮酒的环境与心情上有什么相同和不同的地方？

七、作文

1. 写一篇描写农村风光的作文。自行命题。

21

Bring in the Wine, Please!
将进酒

词汇一

1. **将**, qiāng: 请
2. **进酒**, jìnjiǔ: to fill the wine cup for a guest and urge him to drink it up
3. **得意**, déyì: pleased with oneself or one's situation
4. **莫**, mò: 不要
5. **材**, cái: 才, talent
6. **烹**, pēng: to cook, to boil
7. **宰**, zǎi: to slaughter, to butcher
8. **且**, qiě: for the time being, for the moment
9. **会须**, huìxū: 应当
10. **岑夫子**, Cén fūzi: Cén Xūn 岑勋，李白的朋友 (fl. 735)
11. **丹丘生**, Dānqiū shēng: Yuán Dānqiū 元丹丘，李白的朋友 (fl. 728–ca. 750)
12. **倾耳**, qīng'ěr: to bend the ear, attentively
13. **钟**, zhōng: bell
14. **馔玉**, zhuànyù: to have delicious and sumptuous food
15. **馔**, zhuàn: to eat and drink
16. **足**, zú: enough
17. **贤**, xián: a person of virtue and talent
18. **陈王**, Chén Wáng: Prince of Chen, Cáo Zhí 曹植 (192–232)
19. **昔时**, xīshí: 从前、古时候
20. **平乐**, Pínglè: Pingle Temple, where Cao Zhi held a lavish banquet
21. **恣**, zì: to throw off restraints, to do as one pleases
22. **谑**, xuè: to make jokes
23. **何为**, héwèi: 为什么
24. **言**, yán: 说
25. **径须**, jìngxū: to do anything as one wishes, by all means
26. **沽**, gū: 买
27. **五花马**, wǔhuāmǎ: 毛为五色的好马
28. **千金**, qiānjīn: 一千斤黄金，形容非常贵重的东西
29. **裘**, qiú: 皮衣
30. **儿**, ér: 小孩
31. **将**, jiāng: 拿、取
32. **尔**, ěr: 你
33. **销**, xiāo: to melt, to dispel
34. **万古**, wàngǔ: through the ages

将进酒

君不见黄河之水天上来，奔流到海不复回。
君不见高堂明镜悲白发，朝如青丝暮成雪。
人生得意须尽欢，莫使金尊空对月。
天生我材必有用，　千金散尽还复来。
烹羊宰牛且为乐，会须一饮三百杯。
岑夫子，丹丘生，
将进酒，君莫停。
与君歌一曲，　请君为我倾耳听。
钟鼓馔玉不足贵，但愿长醉不愿醒。
古来圣贤皆寂寞，惟有饮者留其名。
陈王昔时宴平乐，斗酒十千恣欢谑。
主人何为言少钱？径须沽取对君酌。
五花马，千金裘，
呼儿将出换美酒，与尔同销万古愁。

赏析

　　这首诗一开头气势就很大。"天上来"既是指黄河从高处流下，也是指从远处天边奔来。诗人以黄河奔流入海的壮丽景象，比喻时间一去不复返。接下来，诗人以黑发一天变白的夸张描写，引出光阴似箭，人生短暂的感叹。

　　既然岁月易逝、人生如梦、功业难成，何不"一饮三百杯"呢？"人生得意须尽欢"，"得意"在此并不一定指事业上的成功，而是指有开心事，这里指的是朋友欢聚。"天生我材必有用，千金散尽还复来"充分表现了李白的自信与豪放。

　　末句点明喝酒的目的是"与尔同销万古愁"。这个愁是怀才不遇、报国无门的愁。李白在这首诗中，以充沛的激情，唱出了及时行乐、轻视功名富贵的思想。

词汇二

1. **返**, fǎn: 回
2. **光阴**, guāngyīn: time
3. **箭**, jiàn: arrow
4. **岁月**, suìyuè: time, years
5. **逝**, shì: to pass, to die
6. **功业**, gōngyè: exploits, achievements
7. **何不**, hébù: 为什么不
8. **怀才不遇**, huáicái búyù: to have talent but no opportunity to use it
9. **报国**, bàoguó: to dedicate oneself to one's country
10. **充沛**, chōngpèi: plentiful, abundant

练习

一、选择题

1. 这首诗一开头 _____ 就很大。
   - a. 气势
   - b. 气氛
   - c. 气力
   - d. 气味

2. 既然岁月易逝、人生如梦， _____ "一饮三百杯" 呢?
   - a. 为何
   - b. 如何
   - c. 何不
   - d. 何况

3. 这个愁是怀才不遇、 _____ 的愁。
   - a. 光阴似箭
   - b. 人生如梦
   - c. 及时行乐
   - d. 报国无门

4. "天生我材必有用，千金散尽还复来" 充分表现了李白的自信与 _____ 。
   - a. 骄傲
   - b. 豪放
   - c. 兴奋
   - d. 忧愁

二、造句

1. 得意　　2. 光阴　　3. 何不　　4. 怀才不遇　5. 充沛

三、中译英

1. 君不见黄河之水天上来，奔流到海不复回。 君不见高堂明镜悲白发，朝如青丝暮成雪。

2. 人生得意须尽欢，莫使金樽空对月。天生我材必有用，千金散尽还复来。

3. 李白在这首诗中，以充沛的激情，唱出了及时行乐、轻视功名富贵的思想。

四、英译中

1. The poet used the magnificent image of the Yellow River rushing into the sea as a metaphor for time's inexorable passing.

2. The poet used the exaggerated description of the black hair turning to white in one day as a metaphor for time's passing like arrows and the shortness of human life.

3. This poem shows both Li Bai's confidence in his own talent and his sorrow about not being appreciated.

五、回答题

1. 为什么李白说"黄河之水天上来"?

2. "人生得意须尽欢"中的"得意"指的是什么?

3. 陈王是谁?

4. "与尔同销万古愁"说的是什么愁?

六、讨论题

1. 这首诗开头的两个比喻跟诗的主题有什么关系?

2. 李白在这首诗中用了不少夸张的数字,如"千金"、"三百杯"、"斗酒十千"、"千金裘"、"万古愁"。请说明这些数字在诗中的作用。

3. 用下列诗句为例说明李白对饮酒的看法:"人生得意须尽欢,莫使金樽空对月","烹羊宰牛且为乐,会须一饮三百杯","钟鼓馔玉不足贵,但愿长醉不愿醒"。

4. 用下列诗句为例说明李白对金钱的看法:"陈王昔时宴平乐,斗酒十千恣欢谑","主人何为言少钱,径须沽取对君酌","天生我材必有用,千金散尽还复来"。

七、作文

1. 题目:《李白饮酒诗中表现的道家思想》

22

A Brief Biography of Du Fu
杜甫小传

杜工部元稹論云山東人李白亦以文奇取稱時人謂之李杜予觀其壯浪縱恣擺去拘束模寫物象及樂府歌詩誠亦差肩於子美矣至若鋪陳終始排比聲韻大或千言次猶數百詞氣豪邁而風調清深屬對律切而脫棄凡近則李尚不能歷其藩翰況堂奥乎自後屬文者以稹論為是甫有文集六十卷

杜工部

词汇一

1. **书香门第**, shūxiāng méndì: a scholar's family
2. **杜审言**, Dù Shěnyán: 唐朝 诗人 (ca. 645–ca. 708)
3. **吾**, wú: 我 (in classical Chinese)
4. **洛阳**, Luòyáng: a city in Henan 河南 Province
5. **轨迹**, guǐjī: orbit, trajectory
6. **交叉**, jiāochā: to intersect, to cross
7. **一见如故**, yíjiàn rúgù: to feel like old friends at the first meeting
8. **终身**, zhōngshēn: lifelong
9. **一度**, yídù: for a time, once, on one occasion
10. **困**, kùn: to be under siege, to be trapped
11. **跋涉**, báshè: to trudge, to trek
12. **湘江**, Xiāngjiāng: Xiang River, in Hunan Province
13. **动荡**, dòngdàng: turbulence, upheaval
14. **密切**, mìqiè: close, inseparable
15. **相关**, xiāngguān: to be interrelated
16. **忠实**, zhōngshí: faithful
17. **崇高**, chónggāo: lofty, sublime, high
18. **赞扬**, zànyáng: to praise, to speak highly of
19. **肯定**, kěndìng: to affirm
20. **批判**, pīpàn: to criticize
21. **官吏**, guānlì: government officials
22. **腐败**, fǔbài: corruption
23. **关注**, guānzhù: 关心和注意
24. **疾苦**, jíkǔ: suffering, hardship
25. **良心**, liángxīn: conscience

杜甫小传

　　杜甫（712-770），字子美，出生于一个书香门第。祖父杜审言也是有名的诗人，所以杜甫说"诗是吾家事"。杜甫二十三岁时参加科举考试，但失败了。三十二岁时，他在洛阳与李白相识，两颗巨星的轨迹交叉在一起。他们虽然相差十一岁，但一见如故，成为终身好友。公元七百四十六年，他到了长安，在那里住了十年。

　　公元七百五十五年，他终于得到了一个小官的职位。但不久安史之乱就爆发了。叛军攻陷长安后，杜甫一度被困在城内。逃出来后，他在肃宗的朝廷做过一个很短时期的官。公元七百五十九年，杜甫全家经过长途跋涉，到成都定居。杜甫晚年离开成都，准备回到长安去，却不幸病死在湘江中的一条破船上。

　　杜甫艰难困苦的一生，与唐代的社会动荡密切相关。他的诗篇忠实而生动地记录了战争造成的灾难，反映了许多重大的历史事件。杜诗因此被称为"诗史"。

　　杜甫本人则被后人称为"诗圣"。这个崇高的称号当然是对他的诗歌艺术的赞扬，但更主要的是对杜诗的道德力量的肯定。杜甫在他现存的一千四百多首诗中，批判官吏的腐败，关注国家的情况，同情人民生活的疾苦，显示了一个儒家学者的社会良心。

练习

一、选择题

1. 三十二岁时，杜甫在 _____ 与李白相识。
   - a. 洛阳
   - b. 长安
   - c. 成都
   - d. 扬州
2. 杜甫在他的诗中批判了官吏的 _____ 。
   - a. 患难
   - b. 腐败
   - c. 疾苦
   - d. 变化
3. 杜甫的诗显示了一个儒家学者的社会 _____ 。
   - a. 知识
   - b. 良心
   - c. 责任
   - d. 思想

二、造句

1. 交叉   2. 一见如故   3. 终身   4. 一度   5. 跋涉
6. 密切   7. 忠实   8. 批判   9. 疾苦

三、中译英

1. 杜甫对自己的创作上的要求很高，象他自己所说的那样：“语不惊人死不休”。
2. 杜甫的诗语言精练而富有表现力，比如他的诗句“朱门酒肉臭，路有冻死骨”形象地概括出社会上的贫富对立。
3. 李白生前就非常有名；可是杜甫一生穷困，死后名声才慢慢大起来。

四、英译中

1. His poems recorded faithfully and vividly the chaos caused by war, reflecting many momentous historical events. Du Fu's poetry has thus been called "history in verse."
2. Du Fu has earned the title of the "Sage of Poetry." This honorable title is of course in praise of his poetic art, but more importantly, this is the recognition of the moral force of his poems.

3. Du Fu's more than 1,400 surviving poems voice his criticisms of official corruption, concerns for the empire, and intense compassion for dispossessed people, thus manifesting the social conscience of a Confucian scholar.

五、回答题

1. 为什么杜甫说"诗是吾家事"？
2. 杜甫有没有参加过科举考试？
3. 杜甫三十二岁时在哪儿与李白相识？
4. 公元七百四十六年，杜甫到了长安，他在那里住了几年？
5. 杜甫一家经过长途跋涉到哪儿定居下来？
6. 杜甫现存诗多少首？

六、讨论题

1. 为什么杜诗被称为"诗史"？
2. 为什么杜甫被称为"诗圣"？

七、专题研究

1. 李白和杜甫都写了一些寄给对方或关于对方的诗。根据这些诗，作一个关于两人的友谊的报告。（关键词：《鲁郡东石门送杜二甫"》、《沙丘城下寄杜甫》、《戏赠杜甫》、《赠李白》、《春日忆李白》、《梦李白二首》、《天末怀李白》、《冬日有怀李白》、《寄李十二白二十韵》）

23

A Brief Introduction
to War Poetry
战乱诗小序

天寒翠袖薄

词汇一

1. **组成部分**, zǔchéng bùfen: component
2. **组成**, zǔchéng: to form, to compose
3. **类型**, lèixíng: type, mode
4. **战役**, zhànyì: campaign, battle
5. **官军**, guānjūn: government troops
6. **忧虑**, yōulǜ: worry, anxiety
7. **平叛**, píngpàn: 平定叛乱, to suppress a rebellion
8. **战局**, zhànjú: war situation/state
9. **长达**, chángdá: with the great length of
10. **史诗**, shǐshī: epic
11. **征**, zhēng: to journey
12. **典型**, diǎnxíng: model, typical example
13. **吏**, lì: civil officer, clerk
14. **新安**, Xīn'ān: a village in Henan Province
15. **潼关**, Tóngguān: the Tong Pass, in Shaanxi 陕西 Province
16. **石壕**, Shíháo: a village in Henan Province
17. **垂老**, chuílǎo: with old age approaching, in declining years
18. **遭遇**, zāoyù: (bitter) experience
19. **茅屋**, máowū: thatched house
20. **渴望**, kěwàng: to thirst for, to yearn for

小序

战乱诗是杜诗的一个最重要的组成部分，也是杜诗被称为"诗史"的主要原因。杜甫的战乱诗大致可分成以下三个类型。

有些诗记述了当时的一些重大事件和主要战役。杜甫在诗中常常为官军的胜仗而欢呼，为官军的败仗而痛哭。他的很多诗表达了对国事的忧虑和对平叛的希望，有时甚至对战局提出建议。他的长达一百四十行的史诗《北征》就是这类诗的典型。

杜甫更多的诗篇反映了战争给人民带来的苦难生活。这方面的代表作有《三吏》（《新安吏》、《潼关吏》《石壕吏》）和《三别》（《新婚别》、《垂老别》、《无家别》）。

杜甫也写了很多自己家庭在战乱中的遭遇和感受，如他陷在长安时写的《春望》和《月夜》。他在成都写的《茅屋为秋风所破歌》，虽然和战争没有直接关系，但反映了战乱造成的贫困生活和对安定生活的渴望。

练习

一、选择题

1. 杜甫的战乱诗大致可分成三个 _____ 。
      a. 主题   b. 题材
      c. 体裁   d. 类型

2. 有些诗记述了当时的一些重大事件和主要 _____ 。
      a. 战争   b. 战斗
      c. 战役   d. 战场

3. 他的很多诗表达了对国事的 _____ 和对平叛的希望。
      a. 忧虑   b. 渴望
      c. 体会   d. 幻想

4. 他的《北征》是一首长达一百四十行的_____ 。
      a. 诗史   b. 史诗
      c. 事实   d. 时事

二、造句

1. 组成   2. 战役   3. 忧虑   4. 战局   5. 史诗
6. 遭遇   7. 渴望

三、中译英

1. 据史书记载，安史之乱前，全国有九百多万户，安史之乱后，只剩下一百九十三万户，减少了四分之三以上。
2. 杜甫写了很多自己家庭在战乱中的遭遇和感受，反映了战乱造成的苦难和对安定生活的渴望。

四、英译中

1. War poetry is the most important component of Du Fu's works, and is also the major reason why Du Fu's poetry has been called "history in verse."
2. In his poems, Du Fu often hailed the victories of government armies, and lamented their defeats.

3. Some of his poems recorded important events and major battles at the time; others described people's misfortunes during the war.

五、回答题

1. 杜甫的《北征》是一首什么样的诗？它有多少行？
2. 杜甫反映战乱中人民苦难生活的诗有些什么代表作？
3. 杜甫身陷长安时写了些什么诗？

六、讨论题

1. 杜甫的战乱诗大致可分成哪三个类型？请举例说明。

七、专题研究

1. 简单报告一下安史之乱的起因、发展、平定和危害。

24

Moonlit Night
月夜

词汇一

1. **鄜州**, Fūzhōu: a city in today's Shaanxi Province
2. **闺**, guī: 女子的卧室
3. **云鬟**, yúnhuán: beautiful and thick hair (like a cloud)
4. **鬟**, huán: bun of hair
5. **玉**, yù: jade
6. **臂**, bì: arm
7. **倚**, yǐ: to lean on or against
8. **虚**, xū: 空、透明
9. **幌**, huǎng: curtain
10. **痕**, hén: mark, trace

月夜

今夜鄜州月，闺中只独看。
遥怜小儿女，未解忆长安。
香雾云鬟湿，清辉玉臂寒。
何时倚虚幌，双照泪痕干。

赏析

公元七五六年六月，安禄山叛军攻陷长安，杜甫携带妻小逃到鄜州，寄居羌村。七月，肃宗在灵武即位。杜甫在独自前往灵武的途中被叛军俘虏，和难民一起被押送到长安。从七五六年八月到第二年四月，杜甫在沦陷区长安共生活了八个月左右。这是他在那年秋天思念妻子的一首诗。

首联实际上是抒写自己望月思家的心情，但倒过来写想象中妻子在思念诗人。明明是长安之月，却偏偏说"鄜州月"。因为丈夫不在家，所以妻子只能独自望月。

颔联进一步说明首联：妻子的望月，实际上是"忆长安"；儿女还小，不懂得想念父亲，也不会陪妈妈一起望月。

颈联说明妻子望月很久了，以致头发都被雾气打湿了，手臂也冷了。此联融情入景，杜甫把妻子在月光下想念丈夫的形象写得很凄凉也很美丽，表达出他对妻子的深厚的感情。

尾联以问句作结束。"倚虚幌"是两人一起望月的姿态。这联中的"双照"与前三联描写的"独看"相对照，表达了对国家安定、家人团聚的期望。

词汇二

1. **携带**, xiédài: to take along
2. **妻小**, qīxiǎo: wife and children
3. **寄居**, jìjū : to live away from home
4. **羌村**, Qiāngcūn: a village in Fu County of Shaanxi Province
5. **即位**, jíwèi: to ascend the throne
6. **俘虏**, fúlǔ: to capture, to take prisoner
7. **难民**, nànmín: refugee
8. **押送**, yāsòng: to send under escort or guard
9. **沦陷区**, lúnxiànqū: enemy-occupied area
10. **抒写**, shūxiě: to express, to describe
11. **明明**, míngmíng: obviously
12. **偏偏**, piānpiān: (an adverb indicating a sense of obstinate contrariness)
13. **凄凉**, qīliáng: sad, miserable
14. **团聚**, tuánjù: reunion

练习

一、选择题

1. 杜甫在独自前往 _____ 的途中被叛军俘虏。
   - a. 灵武
   - b. 鄜州
   - c. 羌村
   - d. 长安
2. 首联实际上是 _____ 诗人自己望月思家的心情。
   - a. 描写
   - b. 抒写
   - c. 记录
   - d. 叙述
3. 尾联中的"双照"与前三联描写的"独看"相
   _____ 。
   - a. 呼应
   - b. 交流
   - c. 对照
   - d. 联系

二、造句

1. 携带
2. 寄居
3. 俘虏
4. 难民
5. 抒写
6. 明明
7. 偏偏
8. 凄凉
9. 团聚

三、中译英

1. 何时倚虚幌，双照泪痕干。
2. 这首诗从现实中的"独"开始，到希望中的"双"结束，表达了家人分离的痛苦和对团聚的期待。
3. 杜甫的妻子在月光下思念丈夫的形象，既凄凉又美丽，成为战争中人民苦难生活的象征。

四、英译中

1. Du Fu was captured by the rebel army while traveling to Lingwu by himself and was sent under guard to Chang'an together with other refugees.
2. Du Fu lived in enemy-occupied Chang'an for about eight months. He wrote this poem in autumn of that year, when he was missing his wife.
3. The third couplet says that his wife has been watching the moon for a very long time so that her hair is wet by the fog and her arms feel cold.
4. The last couplet expresses the poet's hope for the country's stability and family reunion.

五、回答题

1. 安禄山叛军攻陷长安后，杜甫携带妻小逃到哪儿？
2. 杜甫为什么会被叛军俘虏？
3. 杜甫在沦陷区长安生活了多久？
4. 在这首诗中，杜甫主要思念谁？
5. 杜甫的妻子为什么要望月？
6. 为什么杜甫的儿女还不懂得想念父亲？
7. 你怎么知道杜甫的妻子望月已经望得很久了？

六、讨论题

1. 杜甫这首诗写的是自己的遭遇和感受，但它的意义超出了他的家庭范围。谈谈这首诗的社会意义。
2. 李白的《玉阶怨》也是写一位女子望着月亮在思念心中的人。比较杜甫的《月夜》和李白的《玉阶怨》中两个妇女的形象及她们的思念。

七、作文

1. 写一篇短文讲述战争给人民带来的苦难生活。古今中外的例子都可以用。

25

Facing the Snow
对雪

词汇一

1. **鬼**, guǐ: ghost
2. **吟**, yín: to chant, to recite
3. **薄暮**, bómù: dusk, twilight
4. **回**, huí: whirling
5. **瓢**, piáo: ladle (often made of a dried gourd)
6. **弃**, qì: to throw away, to discard
7. **存**, cún: to exist
8. **数**, shù: 几 (个)
9. **书空**, shūkōng: 用手指在空中写字

对雪

战哭多新鬼，愁吟独老翁。
乱云低薄暮，急雪舞回风。
瓢弃尊无绿，炉存火似红。
数州消息断，愁坐正书空。

赏析

　　这首诗写于七五六年冬天，和《月夜》一样，是杜甫身陷长安时的作品。

　　这年十月，官军接连打了两个大败仗。这首诗的第一句指的就是这事。第二句写自己。杜甫当时四十四岁，但已自称老翁。听到官军战败，只能独自发愁。第三、第四句写"对雪"：窗外乌云密布、大雪飞舞。在这阴沉、寒冷天气，只能借酒浇愁、生火取暖了。但是酒呢？酒瓢扔在一边，酒坛里早就没有绿色的酒了。火呢？炉子虽然还在，但是也没火了，只是在想象中，它还是红的。镜头最后又回到诗人，一个人在用手指在空中写字。"书空"是个典故，说的是晋朝有个人被罢官后，常用手指在空中写"咄咄怪事"四个字。在杜甫看来，官军接连打败仗，不是咄咄怪事吗？

词汇二

1. **老翁**, lǎowēng: old man
2. **发愁**, fāchóu: to worry
3. **乌云密布**, wūyún mìbù: black clouds densely covering the sky
4. **阴沉**, yīnchén: cloudy, gloomy, somber
5. **酒坛**, jiǔtán: wine jug
6. **典故**, diǎngù: allusion
7. **晋朝**, Jìn Cháo: the Jin Dynasty (265–420)
8. **罢官**, bàguān: to be dismissed from office
9. **咄咄怪事**, duōduō guàishì: what a queer story, what a strange phenomenon

练习

一、选择题

1. 杜甫当时四十四岁，但已自称 _____ 。
   - a. 老人
   - b. 老汉
   - c. 老翁
   - d. 老年
2. 听到官军战败，只能独自 _____ 。
   - a. 忧愁
   - b. 发愁
   - c. 浇愁
   - d. 离愁
3. 在这阴沉、寒冷天气，只能 _____ 了。
   - a. 乌云密布
   - b. 大雪飞舞
   - c. 借酒浇愁
   - d. 咄咄怪事
4. 炉子虽然还在，但是也没火了，只是在 _____ 中，它还是红的。
   - a. 理想
   - b. 思想
   - c. 想念
   - d. 想象
5. 晋朝有个人被罢官后，常用 _____ 在空中写"咄咄怪事"四个字。
   - a. 毛笔
   - b. 铅笔
   - c. 钢笔
   - d. 手指

二、造句

1. 发愁　2. 乌云密布　3. 阴沉　4. 典故　5. 咄咄怪事

三、中译英

1. 战哭多新鬼，愁吟独老翁。乱云低薄暮，急雪舞回风。
2. 这首诗的表现方式象是电影镜头由远到近的移动：先是窗外的旷野和大雪，然后是屋内的诗人以及酒坛和火炉。
3. 杜甫这首诗写的是七五六年十月官军大败后他的反应。从这首诗中我们可以体会到为什么杜诗被称作"诗史"了。

四、英译中

1. As when he wrote "Moonlit Night," Du Fu wrote this poem when he was trapped in Chang'an.
2. Du Fu was forty-four at the time, but he already called himself "old man."
3. Having heard that the government army was defeated, Du Fu could only worry in solitude.

五、回答题

1. 这首诗是杜甫在什么时候、什么地方、什么环境下写的？
2. 这首诗的第一句指的是什么事？
3. 杜甫当时几岁？
4. 听到官军战败，杜甫能做什么？
5. 那天的天气怎么样？
6. 杜甫用手指在空中写什么字？

六、讨论题

1. 说说杜甫在长安沦陷区的生活穷困的情况。
2. 官军大败的消息传来以后，杜甫的心情怎么样？请引用诗句并加以说明。

七、作文

1. 写一篇描写雪景的短文。

26

Spring View
春望

词汇一

1. **溅**, jiàn: to splash
2. **恨**, hèn: to hate, to resent
3. **别**, bié: 分别, separation
4. **烽火**, fēnghuǒ: beacon fire
5. **抵**, dǐ: to be equal to
6. **搔**, sāo: to scratch
7. **浑**, hún: 简直、几乎
8. **欲**, yù: 要
9. **胜**, shèng: to be equal or up to (a certain task)
10. **簪**, zān: hairpin (in ancient times, men used hairpins to hold long hair)

春望

国破山河在，城春草木深。
感时花溅泪，恨别鸟惊心。
烽火连三月，家书抵万金。
白头搔更短，浑欲不胜簪。

赏析

　　这首诗写于七五七年春天。冬去春来，杜甫还身陷长安。首句中"国破"既指国家山河破碎，也指国都长安沦陷。安禄山叛军攻破长安后，大肆抢掠，放火烧城，长安成了一片废墟。"山河在"和"国破"成对照，说明大自然的永恒。第二句"城春草木深"进一步发挥：不管人间的苦难，春天来了，草木照样生长。

　　颔联却告诉我们，即使花鸟也是有情的。诗人春望的视野从大到小，由山河、草木看到了近处的花鸟。"花溅泪"，是谁的泪？可有多种解释。一种是花的泪。杜甫在春望时看到花瓣上的晨露或雨水，觉得花在哭。一种是诗人的泪。诗人伤心之极，见花落泪。一种是苦难人民的泪。这些解释可以结合在一起，可见"花溅泪"三个字的内容多么丰富。"鸟惊心"也可做相似的解释。

　　颈联紧承上联。"烽火"扣"感时"，"家书"扣"恨别"，极写战争持续时间之久，人民蒙受苦难之重。尾联以一个满头白发的老人形象作结束。

词汇二

1. **破碎**, pòsuì: tattered, broken
2. **大肆**, dàsì : without restraint, wantonly
3. **抢掠**, qiǎnglüè: to loot, to sack
4. **废墟**, fèixū: ruins
5. **照样**, zhàoyàng: all the same, as before
6. **发挥**, fāhuī: to develop (an idea, a theme, etc.), to elaborate
7. **花瓣**, huābàn: petal
8. **承**, chéng: to continue, to carry on
9. **扣**, kòu: to refer to, to button up
10. **极**, jí: extremely, to a great extent
11. **蒙受**, méngshòu: to suffer, to sustain

练习

一、选择题

1. 首句中"国破"既指国家山河破碎，也指国都长安
_____ 。
  a. 沦陷   b. 失败
  c. 抢掠   d. 俘虏

2. 安禄山叛军攻破长安后，放火烧城，长安成了一片
_____ 。
  a. 战场   b. 废墟
  c. 烽火   d. 战局

3. "山河在"和"国破"成对照，说明大自然的
_____ 。
  a. 长远   b. 长久
  c. 永恒   d. 永远

4. 不管人间多么苦难，春天来了，草木 _____ 生长。
  a. 尽情   b. 大肆
  c. 偏偏   d. 照样

5. 这些解释可以结合在一起，可见"花溅泪"三个字的内
容多么 _____ 。
  a. 充沛   b. 豪放
  c. 丰富   d. 巨大

二、造句

1. 破碎 2. 大肆 3. 废墟 4. 永恒 5. 照样
6. 发挥 7. 蒙受

三、中译英

1. 国破山河在，城春草木深。感时花溅泪，恨别鸟惊心。
2. 看到《春望》、《月夜》、《对雪》这些诗题，一般人都会想到美丽的自然景色，可是杜甫却在诗中写了战争造成的破坏。

3. 残酷的战争造成很多家庭妻离子散。杜甫的《春望》和《月夜》是这种悲惨的情况的真实写照。

四、英译中

1. After the rebel army took Chang'an, they sacked the city and burned it. Chang'an became a ruin.
2. "Mountains and rivers remaining" contrasts with "nation shattered," telling of the perpetuity of nature.
3. Despite the sufferings of the human world, when spring comes, grass and trees still grow as usual.

五、回答题

1. 首句中"国破"指的是什么?
2. "山河在"和"国破"成对照,说明什么?
3. "花溅泪",是谁的泪?可有哪三种解释?
4. 这首诗是怎么结束的?

六、讨论题

1. 春天万物生长,一般的诗人都会描写欣欣向荣的景色和喜悦的心情。杜甫的《春望》却写了完全不同景色和心情。分析诗中春天的景色和诗人的心情之间的互动。
2. 《月夜》、《对雪》、《春望》这三首诗都是杜甫身陷长安的时候写的。比较这三首诗写作的季节、景色、思想内容和写作手法。

七、作文

1. 写一篇题为《春望》的短文。

27

Qiang Village
羌村

词汇一

1. **峥嵘**, zhēngróng: lofty and steep (used here to describe the shape of clouds)
2. **赤**, chì: 红
3. **日脚**, rìjiǎo: sun beams radiating through the clouds
4. **柴门**, cháimén: door of brushwood
5. **柴**, chái: firewood, brushwood
6. **雀**, què: sparrow
7. **噪**, zào: to chirp
8. **至**, zhì: 到
9. **孥**, nú: children
10. **拭**, shì: to wipe
11. **遭**, zāo: to meet with (disaster, misfortune)
12. **飘荡**, piāodàng: to drift about
13. **偶然**, ǒurán: fortuitous, by chance
14. **遂**, suì: to fulfill (a wish)
15. **亦**, yì: 也、又
16. **嘘唏**, xūxī: to sob
17. **阑**, lán: late
18. **秉**, bǐng: to hold
19. **烛**, zhú: candle
20. **梦寐**, mèngmèi: dream

羌村

峥嵘赤云西，日脚下平地。
柴门鸟雀噪，归客千里至。
妻孥怪我在，惊定还拭泪。
世乱遭飘荡，生还偶然遂。
邻人满墙头，感叹亦嘘唏。
夜阑更秉烛，相对如梦寐。

赏析

　　这首诗是七五七年秋天杜甫回家探亲所写。这是一首叙事诗，语言朴素，感情真挚，写诗人刚到家时与妻子相见的惊喜交集的情景。

　　头四句写诗人到家时，秋天傍晚的乡村景色，有声（鸟噪）有色（赤云），像一幅农村秋景图。"千里至"三字概括了路途中多少艰辛，又流露出终于归来的无限喜悦。

　　中间六句写夫妻相见和邻里隔墙观望的情景。其中"妻孥怪我在，惊定还拭泪"两句写相见时妻子的情态，传神逼真。"怪我在"说明很多人都已不在人世了。一个"怪"字写出了妻子惊讶的神情。古代农家常有围墙小院，由于墙矮，邻人能隔墙相望。左邻右舍看到诗人全家团聚时大喜大悲的样子，不便进来相劝，只能在墙外"嘘唏"。这两句语言明白如话，场景却极为生动。

　　最后两句写直到半夜，夫妻还相对如梦，不敢信以为真。

词汇二

1. **探亲**, tànqīn: to visit one's family
2. **叙事诗**, xùshìshī: narrative poem
3. **朴素**, pǔsù: simple, plain
4. **真挚**, zhēnzhì: sincere, cordial
5. **惊喜交集**, jīngxǐ jiāojí: mixed feelings of surprise and joy
6. **艰辛**, jiānxīn: hardship
7. **情态**, qíngtài: spirit and manner
8. **传神**, chuánshén: vivid
9. **逼真**, bīzhēn: lifelike
10. **惊讶**, jīngyà: surprising
11. **左邻右舍**, zuǒlín yòushě: 邻居们

练习

一、选择题

1. 这是一首叙事诗,语言 _____ ,感情真挚。
   - a. 简单
   - b. 热情
   - c. 朴素
   - d. 激烈
2. 一个"怪"字写出了妻子 _____ 的神情。
   - a. 惊讶
   - b. 悲伤
   - c. 艰辛
   - d. 嘘唏
3. 最后两句写夫妻 _____ ,不敢信以为真。
   - a. 隔墙观望
   - b. 惊喜交集
   - c. 相对如梦
   - d. 伤心落泪

二、造句

1. 偶然
2. 探亲
3. 朴素
4. 艰辛
5. 情态
6. 逼真
7. 传神
8. 惊讶

三、中译英

1. 妻孥怪我在,惊定还拭泪。
2. 夜阑更秉烛,相对如梦寐。
3. 安史之乱中,很多地方十室九空。活着的人相见,会觉得很偶然,象在梦中一样。

四、英译中

1. This poem was written in 757 when Du Fu returned home after a long and hard journey during wartime.
2. This is a narrative poem and the language is quite simple and vivid.
3. It describes the scene when the poet had just arrived home and rejoined his wife with mixed feelings of surprise and joy.

五、回答题

1. 这首诗的语言有什么特色?
2. 这首诗写的是什么样的情景?

3. 头四句写的是什么景色?
4. 哪两句写出了相见时妻子的情态?
5. "邻人满墙头"是个什么样的场景?

六、讨论题
1. "妻孥怪我在"中的"怪"字说明了什么情况?
2. 这是一首叙事诗,写得很简洁。根据诗中描写的情景,
写出诗人和妻子之间的对话,并在班上表演。

七、作文
1. 题目:《重逢》。

28

The Officers of Shihao Village
石壕吏

词汇一

1. 投 (宿), tóusù: to seek temporary lodging
2. 逾, yú: to pass over, to scale (a wall)
3. 走, zǒu: 跑
4. 呼, hū: 大声叫
5. 一何, yìhé: 多么
6. 怒, nù: angry
7. 前, qián: 走上前去
8. 致词, zhìcí: 讲话
9. 男, nán: 儿子
10. 邺城, Yèchéng: a city in today's An'yang City in Henan Province
11. 戍, shù: to garrison
12. 附, fù: 带, (to ask someone) to take, to attach to
13. 书, shū: 信
14. 偷生, tōushēng: to live an ignoble life
15. 已, yǐ: to cease, to end
16. 矣, yǐ: 了 (an auxiliary word in classical Chinese that indicates mood)
17. 乳, rǔ: 奶, breast
18. 完, wán: complete, intact
19. 妪, yù: 老年妇人
20. 衰, shuāi: weak, feeble
21. 应, yìng: to respond to (a call for recruits)
22. 河阳, Héyáng: a city in today's Henan Province
23. 役, yì: 战役, battle
24. 犹, yóu: 还
25. 得, dé: 能
26. 炊, chuī: to cook a meal
27. 绝, jué: to be finished
28. 泣, qì: 低声哭
29. 幽咽, yōuyè: 低声哭泣
30. 登前途, dēng qiántú: to start off on a journey, to set out

石壕吏

暮投石壕村，有吏夜捉人。
老翁逾墙走，老妇出看门。
吏呼一何怒，妇啼一何苦。
听妇前致词，三男邺城戍。
一男附书至，二男新战死。
存者且偷生，死者长已矣。
室中更无人，惟有乳下孙。
有孙母未去，出入无完裙。
老妪力虽衰，请从吏夜归。
急应河阳役，犹得备晨炊。
夜久语声绝，如闻泣幽咽。
天明登前途，独与老翁别。

赏析

　　这也是一首叙事诗。首联直接进入主题。"有吏夜捉人"是一篇的纲领。差吏黑夜捉人，是想趁人不备。"听妇前致词"以下十三句是老妇的话，可分成三层。前五句为第一层，叙述"三男"的遭遇。得不到差吏的同情，她在接着的四句中描写家中困境。仍得不到差吏的谅解，老妇只能在接下的四句中提出自己去河阳前线服役。最后四句是尾声，告诉我们老妇已被差吏抓走。

　　这首诗全篇句句叙事，无抒情、无议论，但深刻地揭露了当时的兵役制度的罪恶，反映了人民在战乱年代的悲惨遭遇。清朝学者仇兆鳌对老妇一家的命运作了很好的概括："三男戍，二男死，孙方乳，媳无裙，翁逾墙，妇夜往，一家之中，父子、兄弟、祖孙、姑媳，惨酷至此，民不聊生极矣。"

词汇二

1. **纲领**, gānglǐng: guiding principle
2. **差吏**, chāilì: civil officer, clerk
3. **趁人不备**, chènrén búbèi: to catch people unaware
4. **趁**, chèn: to take advantage of
5. **困境**, kùnjìng: difficult situation
6. **谅解**, liàngjiě: understanding, forgiveness
7. **服役**, fúyì: to enlist in the army
8. **尾声**, wěishēng: epilogue, ending, (music) coda
9. **议论**, yìlùn: comments, discussions
10. **兵役**, bīngyì: military service
11. **罪恶**, zuì'è: crime, evil
12. **仇兆鳌**, Qiú Zhào'áo: a Qing Dynasty scholar (1638–1713)
13. **命运**, mìngyùn: destiny, fate
14. **概括**, gàikuò: summary
15. **方**, fāng: 刚
16. **媳**, xí: daughter-in-law
17. **姑**, gū: mother-in-law
18. **惨**, cǎn: miserable, tragic
19. **酷**, kù: cruel
20. **民不聊生**, mín bù liáoshēng: people have no means of livelihood

练习

一、选择题

1. 差吏黑夜捉人，是想 _____ 。
  a. 乘人不备   b. 民不聊生
  c. 大肆抢掠   d. 苦难深重

2. 老妇在接着的四句中描写家中的 _____ 。
  a. 遭遇   b. 情况
  c. 忧虑   d. 困境

3. 老妇只能提出自己去河阳前线 _____ 。
  a. 作战   b. 打仗
  c. 做饭   d. 劳动

4. 这首诗深刻地 _____ 了当时的兵役制度的罪恶。
  a. 反映   b. 概括
  c. 说明   d. 揭露

二、造句

1. 困境 2. 谅解 3. 尾声 4. 议论 5. 罪恶
6. 命运 7. 概括 8. 民不聊生

三、中译英

1. 一男附书至，二男新战死。存者且偷生，死者长已矣。
2. 室中更无人，惟有乳下孙。有孙母未去，出入无完裙。
3. 这首诗在结构上很有特色。全诗根据时间顺序展开描写，由日暮到天明，讲了一个差吏捉人的故事，揭露了兵役制度的罪恶。

四、英译中

1. The old woman told of what became of her three sons and the difficult situation of her family, but she still could not get the officers' sympathy.
2. This poem deeply exposes the evils of the draft system at the time.
3. Qing scholar Qiu Zhao'ao summarized well the miserable life of the old woman's family.

五、回答题

1. 差吏为什么要黑夜捉人？
2. 得不到差吏的同情，老妇只能怎么做？
3. "夜久语声绝，如闻泣幽咽"，诗人听到谁在哭泣？
4. 这首诗揭露了什么？
5. 清朝学者仇兆鳌是怎样概括老妇一家的悲惨命运的？

六、讨论题

1. 讲一讲老妇一家的悲惨故事和每个人的命运。
2. 诗人听到的应是老妇和差吏的对话，但他在诗中只写了老妇的话，没写差吏的话。差吏凶狠的样子应该是可以想象的。学生两人一组预习、表演老妇和差吏的对话。
3. "啼"、"哭"、"泣"、"幽咽"、"嘘唏"都是形容哭泣的词，但在声音大小和悲伤程度上有所不同。请具体解释并用这五个词各造一个句子。
4. 这首诗的押韵有什么特点？对诗歌的叙述起了什么作用？

七、专题研究

1. 杜甫的这首《石壕吏》和《新安吏》、《潼关吏》一起被称为"三吏"。介绍一下另外两首诗的主要内容。

29

Newlyweds' Farewell
新婚別

词汇一

1. 菟丝, tùsī: dodder
2. 蓬, péng: fleabane
3. 麻, má: hemp
4. 引, yǐn: to draw, to stretch
5. 蔓, màn: tendril, creeper
6. 故, gù: 所以，因此
7. 征夫, zhēngfū: 战士, soldier
8. 结发, jiéfà: usually, 结发夫妻: husband and wife of the first marriage
9. 席, xí: a mat, especially a straw mat
10. 无乃, wúnǎi: 难道不是
11. 匆忙, cōngmáng: hastily, hurriedly
12. 赴, fù: 去，到
13. 妾, qiè: concubine (in old China, a term used by a wife to refer to herself when speaking to her husband)
14. 身, shēn: 身分, status, identity
15. 未, wèi: 还没有
16. 何以, héyǐ: 拿什么，怎么能
17. 拜, bài: to perform obeisance
18. 姑嫜, gūzhāng: 公婆, in-laws
19. 归, gūi: (said of a woman) marriage
20. 将, jiāng: 跟随
21. 沉痛, chéntòng: deeply grieved
22. 迫, pò: to press
23. 中肠, zhōngcháng: deep inside
24. 肠, cháng: gut, intestines
25. 誓, shì: to vow, to swear
26. 形势, xíngshì: situation
27. 反, fǎn: on the contrary, instead
28. 苍黄, cānghuáng: panic, same as 仓皇
29. 勿, wù: 不要
30. 事, shì: 从事, to be engaged in (a career)
31. 戎行, rónghàng: 军队
32. 兵气, bīngqì: army morale
33. 恐, kǒng: probably, perhaps (with reference to an unpleasant fact)
34. 扬, yáng: to raise, to run high
35. 嗟, jiē: to sigh, to lament
36. 贫, pín: 穷
37. 致, zhì: to achieve, to attain
38. 襦, rú: a short coat, a short top garment
39. 裳, cháng: bottom garment, dress
40. 施, shī: to use, to apply
41. 红妆, hóngzhuāng: makeup
42. 仰, yǎng: face upward
43. 翔, xiáng: 飞
44. 人事, rénshì: human affairs
45. 错迕, cuòwù: disorderly and adverse

新婚别

菟丝附蓬麻，引蔓故不长。
嫁女与征夫，不如弃路旁。
结发为妻子，席不暖君床。
暮婚晨告别，无乃太匆忙。
君行虽不远，守边赴河阳。
妾身未分明，何以拜姑嫜。
父母养我时，日夜令我藏。
生女有所归，鸡狗亦得将。
君今往死地，沉痛迫中肠。
誓欲随君去，形势反苍黄。
勿为新婚念，努力事戎行。
妇人在军中，兵气恐不扬。
自嗟贫家女，久致罗襦裳。
罗襦不复施，对君洗红妆。
仰视百鸟飞，大小必双翔。
人事多错迕，与君永相望。

赏析

这也是一首控诉兵役制度、反映人民悲惨生活的诗。这首诗是用第一人称写的。在结婚的第二天早上，丈夫就要应征赴河阳前线，整首诗是妻子的沉痛的诉说。

诗的头四句和末四句各是一个比喻。开头的比喻说明女主人公的不幸，结尾的比喻说明她对爱情的坚贞。中间二十四句是全诗的中心，是女主人公诉说自己在生离死别时的痛苦复杂的心情。全诗语言朴素自然、明白如话，着重于人物的心理刻画，既表现了女主人公对丈夫的深挚的爱，又抒写了她渴望平定叛乱的心情，表现了她以大局为重的崇高品质。

词汇二

1. **控诉**, kòngsù: to denounce, to condemn
2. **第一人称**, dìyī rénchēng: the first person
3. **应征**, yìngzhēng: to be recruited
4. **诉说**, sùshuō: to tell, to recount
5. **末**, mò: end
6. **主人公**, zhǔréngōng: protagonist
7. **坚贞**, jiānzhēn: faithful
8. **生离死别**, shēnglí sǐbié: to part forever
9. **着重**, zhuózhòng: to empahsize
10. **刻画**, kèhuà: to depict, to portray
11. **深挚**, shēnzhì: deep and sincere
12. **大局**, dàjú: overall situation
13. **品质**, pǐnzhì: character, quality

练习

一、选择题

1. 整首诗是妻子的 _____ 的诉说。
   a. 沉痛　　　　　　　　b. 不幸
   c. 匆忙　　　　　　　　d. 深挚

2. 结尾的比喻说明她对爱情的 _____ 。
   a. 坚决　　　　　　　　b. 坚贞
   c. 坚持　　　　　　　　d. 坚强

3. 女主人公诉说自己在 _____ 时的痛苦复杂的心情。
   a. 乌云密布　　　　　　b. 烽火连天
   c. 生离死别　　　　　　d. 惊喜交集

4. 全诗语言朴素自然、明白如话，着重于人物的心理
   _____ 。
   a. 揭露　　　　　　　　b. 表现
   c. 诉说　　　　　　　　d. 刻画

二、造句

1. 匆忙　　2. 沉痛　　3. 形势　　4. 控诉　　5. 诉说
6. 主人公　7. 坚贞　　8. 刻画　　9. 深挚

三、中译英

1. 仰视百鸟飞，大小必双翔。人事多错迕，与君永相望。
2. 读完这首诗，女主人公的形象出现在我们面前。她那真挚而深情的表白，唤起我们深深的同情。
3. 在古代，女人"嫁鸡随鸡，嫁狗随狗"，所以丈夫的安危是决定妻子的命运的关键。

四、英译中

1. This is also a poem that condemns the draft system and describes people's miserable lives.
2. The metaphor in the beginning tells of the misfortune of the female protagonist, and the metaphor at the end shows her faithfulness to her husband.

3. The twenty-four lines in the middle part are the central focus of the poem; the bride tells of her painful and complex feelings at this moment of parting forever.

五、回答题

1. 这首诗是用第几人称写的？
2. 在结婚的第二天早上，丈夫就要去哪里？
3. 这首诗的语言有什么特点？
4. 杜甫写出了女主人公的什么感情和品质？

六、讨论题

1. 这首诗和《石壕吏》都是对征兵制度的控诉。结合这两首诗，说明当时的征兵制度的残酷。
2. 请说明这首诗开头和结尾的两个比喻的作用。

七、专题研究

1. 中国古代的婚姻习俗。（关键词：媒人、彩礼、花轿、喜酒、洞房）

30

A Beautiful Lady
佳人

词汇一

1. **佳人**, jiārén: 美女
2. **绝代**, juédài: 当代最好的
3. **谷**, gǔ: valley
4. **云**, yún: 说
5. **良家子**, liángjiāzǐ : children of good parentage
6. **零落**, língluò: withered and fallen
7. **关中**, guānzhōng: Chang'an area
8. **丧败**, sàngbài: 失败
9. **杀戮**, shālù: massacre, slaughter
10. **论**, lùn: to discuss, to talk about
11. **骨肉**, gǔròu: flesh and blood, kindred
12. **世情**, shìqíng: human feelings
13. **恶**, wù: 厌恶, to detest
14. **歇**, xiē: 停歇, to stop
15. **转烛**, zhuǎnzhú: (a metaphor for quick changes)
16. **夫婿**, fūxù: husband
17. **轻薄儿**, qīngbó'ér: a frivolous youngster, a coxcomb
18. **轻薄**, qīngbó: frivolous, philandering
19. **新人**, xīnrén: a new wife (in reference to the original wife)
20. **合昏**, héhūn: also called 夜合花, which opens in the morning and closes in the evening
21. **尚**, shàng: 尚且, even
22. **鸳鸯**, yuānyang: Mandarin ducks (symbolic of an affectionate couple)
23. **那**, nǎ: 哪
24. **泉**, quán: spring
25. **浊**, zhuó: turbid, muddy
26. **侍婢**, shìbì: maidservant
27. **珠**, zhū: pearl
28. **牵**, qiān: to pull
29. **补**, bǔ: to mend, to repair
30. **摘**, zhāi: to pick, to pluck
31. **插**, chā: to stick in, to insert
32. **柏**, bǎi: cypress
33. **动**, dòng: often, easily
34. **盈**, yíng: 满
35. **掬**, jū: to hold with both hands, a double handful
36. **翠**, cuì: emerald green, bluish green
37. **修**, xiū: 长

佳人

绝代有佳人，幽居在空谷。
自云良家子，零落依草木。
关中昔丧败，兄弟遭杀戮。
官高何足论，不得收骨肉。
世情恶衰歇，万事随转烛。
夫婿轻薄儿，新人已如玉。
合昏尚知时，鸳鸯不独宿。
但见新人笑，那闻旧人哭。
在山泉水清，出山泉水浊。
侍婢卖珠回，牵萝补茅屋。
摘花不插发，采柏动盈掬。
天寒翠袖薄，日暮倚修竹。

赏析

　　全诗二十四句可分为三段。前八句为第一段，叙述安史之乱中佳人家庭的不幸遭遇。中间八句为第二段，是佳人被丈夫遗弃后的内心痛苦的表白。最后八句为第三段，描写佳人在艰难困苦中坚定不移的高贵品质。

　　第三段中，"在山泉水清，出山泉水浊"比喻佳人以前和现在不同环境中的生活和社会地位。"侍婢"两句写佳人的清贫而高洁的生活。"摘花不插发"表现了她被遗弃之后的寂寞与痛苦。"采柏动盈掬"是说她因贫穷而吃柏树的果实。最后两句描写了佳人的形象。"天寒翠袖薄"，可见衣服不足以御寒。"日暮倚修竹"不仅是一幅优美的图画，还有着深刻的含义：竹子能经风霜而终年长绿，不正是佳人的坚贞精神的象征吗？

词汇二

1. **遗弃**, yíqì: to abandon, to forsake
2. **表白**, biǎobái: to express or state clearly, to clarify
3. **坚定不移**, jiāndìng bùyí: firm and unshakable
4. **清贫**, qīngpín: poor and virtuous
5. **高洁**, gāojié: noble and pure
6. **寂寞**, jìmò: lonely
7. **御寒**, yùhán: to keep out the cold
8. **御**, yù: to resist, to keep out
9. **不仅**, bùjǐn: not only
10. **深刻**, shēnkè: deep, profound
11. **终年**, zhōngnián: all year round

练习

一、选择题

1. 第三段描写佳人在 _____ 中坚定不移的高贵品质。
   - a. 民不聊生
   - b. 生离死别
   - c. 艰难困苦
   - d. 天寒日暮

2. "侍婢" 两句写佳人的 _____ 而高洁的生活。
   - a. 朴素
   - b. 清贫
   - c. 痛苦
   - d. 惨酷

3. "摘花不插发" 表现了她被 _____ 之后的寂寞与痛苦。
   - a. 遗留
   - b. 遗忘
   - c. 遗弃
   - d. 遗漏

4. 竹子能经风霜而终年长绿，不正是佳人的坚贞精神的 _____ 吗？
   - a. 比喻
   - b. 概括
   - c. 描写
   - d. 象征

二、造句

1. 遗弃　　2. 表白　　3. 坚定不移　　4. 清贫　　5. 寂寞
6. 不仅　　7. 深刻　　8. 终年

三、中译英

1. 在山泉水清，出山泉水浊。侍婢卖珠回，牵萝补茅屋。
2. 摘花不插发，采柏动盈掬。天寒翠袖薄，日暮倚修竹。
3. 杜甫这首诗中的 "佳人" 出身在一个高官的家庭，可是也家破人亡，可见安史之乱的破坏性之大。

四、英译中

1. The first paragraph tells of the misfortunes of the beautiful lady's family.
2. The eight lines in the middle express the distress of the beautiful lady after being abandoned by her husband.

3. The third paragraph describes the beautiful lady's character of standing firm during hardship.

五、回答题

1. 这首诗可分成几段？每段几句？每段主要讲什么？
2. 家人的父亲是做个什么样的人？你怎么知道？
3. "日暮倚修竹"这句诗有着什么深刻的含义？

六、讨论题

1. 这首诗中充满了比喻和象征。找出运用这些手法的诗句，并加以说明。
2. 杜甫描写了佳人生活的贫穷，请举例说明。
3.《佳人》与《新婚别》都是一个女子讲述自己在战乱中的不幸遭遇。比较这两个悲剧的相同和不同之处。

七、专题研究

1. 中国人很喜欢竹子，因为它能经风霜而终年长绿。清代的画家郑板桥就以写竹、画竹著名。请举例说明郑板桥对竹子的形态和精神的描写。

31

Song: My Thatched Cottage Torn by the Autumn Wind
茅屋为秋风所破歌

词汇一

1. 号, háo: to howl, to yell
2. 卷, juǎn: to sweep off
3. 洒, sǎ: to spray
4. 罥, juàn: to entwine, to wind
5. 梢, shāo: the tip of a branch
6. 塘, táng: pool, pond
7. 坳, ào: depression, low-lying land
8. 欺, qī: to bully, to take advantage of
9. 忍, rěn: to be hardhearted enough to
10. 盗, dào: thief, robber
11. 贼, zéi: thief
12. 公然, gōngrán: openly, brazenly
13. 唇, chún: lip
14. 焦, jiāo: burnt
15. 燥, zào: dry
16. 俄顷, éqǐng: in a moment
17. 漠漠, mòmò: misty and vast
18. 衾, qīn: quilt
19. 娇, jiāo: delicate, pampered
20. 恶卧, èwò: to not sleep peacefully
21. 里, lǐ: lining
22. 裂, liè: to split open
23. 丧乱, sāngluàn: disturbance, turmoil
24. 何由, héyóu: 怎么才能
25. 彻, chè: through
26. 安, ān: 怎么
27. 厦, shà: a tall building
28. 庇, bì: to shelter, to protect

29. 寒士, hánshì: a poor scholar
30. 欢颜, huānyán: happy (face)
31. 呜呼, wūhū: alas
32. 突兀, tūwù: sudden
33. 庐, lú: hut, cottage
34. 冻, dòng: to freeze, to feel very cold

茅屋为秋风所破歌

八月秋高风怒号，卷我屋上三重茅。
茅飞度江洒江郊，高者挂罥长林梢，下者飘转沉塘坳。
南村群童欺我老无力，忍能对面为盗贼。
公然抱茅入竹去，唇焦口燥呼不得，归来倚杖自叹息。
俄顷风定云墨色，秋天漠漠向昏黑。
布衾多年冷似铁，娇儿恶卧踏里裂。
床头屋漏无干处，雨脚如麻未断绝。
自经丧乱少睡眠，长夜沾湿何由彻。
安得广厦千万间，大庇天下寒士俱欢颜，风雨不动安如山。
呜呼！何时眼前突兀见此屋，吾庐独破受冻死亦足。

赏析

公元七五九年底，杜甫经过长途跋涉，到达成都。在朋友的帮助下，他盖起了自己的茅屋。可是第二年八月，就遭遇了一场暴风雨。按照中国农历，八月是秋天的第二个月。

全篇可分为四段。前五句写狂风卷走屋顶茅草的情景。次五句写顽童抢走茅草的场面。群童抱茅而去，也因饥寒所迫，反映了广大人民的贫困。接下来的八句写连夜秋雨、床头屋漏。中国有句俗语："屋漏偏遭连夜雨"，杜甫经历的正是这样的苦况。

最后五句由现实写到理想，由叙事转入抒情。诗人由自己的狼狈处境联想到世上的穷苦读书人，发出"安得广厦千万间，大庇天下寒士俱欢颜"的强烈呼声。最后两个长句"何时眼前突兀见此屋，吾庐独破受冻死亦足"进一步说明为了这个理想能实现，自己甘愿作出牺牲，表现了诗人崇高的思想境界。

杜甫的这首诗对后人影响很大。唐朝诗人白居易（722-846）写道："安得万里裘，盖裹周四垠。稳暖皆如我，天下无寒人"（《新制布裘》）。宋朝诗人和政治家王安石（1021-86）写道："宁令吾庐独破受冻死，不忍四海赤子寒嗖嗖"（《子美画像》）。他们都继承和发扬了杜甫的关心人民疾苦的精神。

词汇二

1. **盖**, gài: to build (a house)
2. **顽童**, wántóng: naughty child
3. **场面**, chǎngmiàn: scene, setting
4. **俗语**, súyǔ: common saying, folk adage
5. **苦况**, kǔkuàng: miserable situation
6. **狼狈**, lángbèi: in a difficult, awkward position
7. **处境**, chǔjìng: (unfavorable) situation
8. **联想**, liánxiǎng: to think of in connection (with the aforementioned)

9. **呼声**, hūshēng: voice (of a strong opinion)

10. **甘愿**, gānyuàn: willingly

11. **牺牲**, xīshēng: to sacrifice

12. **境界**, jìngjiè: realm (of thought, ideal)

13. **白居易**, Bái Jūyì: 唐代诗人 (772–846)

14. **裹**, guǒ: to bind, to wrap

15. **周**, zhōu: circumference, circuit

16. **垠**, yín: boundary, limit

17. **稳**, wěn: smooth and steady, peaceful

18. **王安石**, Wáng Ānshí: 宋代 诗人、政治家 (1021–86)

19. **赤子**, chìzǐ: newborn baby; common people

20. **嗖嗖**, sōusōu: whiz-whiz (onomatopoeia)

21. **继承**, jìchéng: to inherit, to carry on

22. **发扬**, fāyáng: to develop, to carry on

练习

一、选择题

1. 按照中国农历，八月是秋天的第 _____ 个月。

    a. 一   **b.** 二

    c. 三   **d.** 四

2. 屋漏 _____ 遭连夜雨。

    a. 也   **b.** 却

    c. 偏   **d.** 还

3. 诗人由自己的狼狈处境 _____ 到世上的穷苦读书人。

    a. 想象   **b.** 想念

    c. 联想   **d.** 思想

4. 这首诗表现了诗人崇高的思想 _____ 。

    a. 情景   **b.** 处境

    c. 场面   **d.** 境界

二、造句

1. 场面   2. 俗语   3. 偏   4. 狼狈   5. 处境   6. 联想

7. 呼声   8. 甘愿   9. 牺牲   10. 境界   11. 继承   12. 疾苦

三、中译英

1. 安得广厦千万间，大庇天下寒士俱欢颜，风雨不动安如山。呜呼！何时眼前突兀见此屋，吾庐独破受冻死亦足。

2. 杜甫到成都后，总算有了一个家。可是，没过多久，一场暴风卷走了屋顶的茅草。随之而来的是连夜秋雨，床头屋漏。

3. 中国有句俗语："屋漏偏遭连夜雨"，杜甫经历的正是这样的苦况。

四、英译中

1. After arriving in Chengdu, Du Fu built his own thatched house with the help of his friends.

2. The poet was willing to sacrifice his own interests for the realization of his dream.

3. This poem of Du Fu exerted great influence on later people. Tang poet Bai Juyi and Song poet Wang Anshi both wrote similar lines to express their concern for people's hardships.

五、回答题

1. 杜甫怎样才能盖起自己的茅屋？

2. 为什么那些顽童要抢走杜甫的茅草？

3. "屋漏偏遭连夜雨"这句俗语是什么意思？

4. 诗人由自己的狼狈处境联想到什么人？

5. 哪两位诗人继承了杜甫关心人民疾苦的精神，写了跟这首诗类似的诗句？

六、讨论题

1. 根据这首诗，具体地描述杜甫的穷苦生活。

2. 在这首诗的结尾，杜甫表达了一种什么思想？结合他的"诗圣"的称号来讨论。

七、作文

1. 题目：《读杜甫〈茅屋为秋风所破歌〉有感》

32

Writing Down my Thoughts
at Night on the Road
旅夜书怀

词汇一

1. **书**, shū: 写
2. **危**, wēi: 高
3. **樯**, qiáng: mast
4. **阔**, kuò: wide, broad, vast
5. **涌**, yǒng: to gush, to surge, to bob
6. **岂**, qǐ: 难道
7. **著**, zhù: outstanding, notable, famed
8. **休**, xiū: to stop, to cease
9. **飘**, piāo: to flutter
10. **沙鸥**, shā'ōu: *海鸥*, sea gull

旅夜书怀

细草微风岸，危樯独夜舟。
星垂平野阔，月涌大江流。
名岂文章著？官应老病休。
飘飘何所似，天地一沙鸥。

赏析

公元七六五年，杜甫率家离开成都草堂，乘舟东下，本篇就是这次旅途中的作品。

前四句写旅夜，后四句写书怀。一、二句写近景，寓情于景。"细草微风岸"显示渺小，"危樯独夜舟"流露孤独，都是诗人当时的心境。三、四句写远景，气势阔大，与首联成对照。这两句的妙处在于因果倒装。"星垂平野阔"：因为"平野阔"，才会觉得天边的星星垂下来；"月涌大江流"：因为"大江流"，才会觉得月亮在河中的倒影在涌动。

在这深沉的旅夜中，诗人思绪万千。"名岂文章著"是个反问句，文章泛指包括诗歌在内的写作：难道写作会给我带来名声吗？答案是否定的。杜甫在生前并非很有名，直到死后名声才越来越大。尾联用"天地一沙鸥"的形象来比喻自己的流离漂泊，情景交融，把"旅夜"和"书怀"结合起来。

词汇二

1. **率**, shuài: 带
2. **寓**, yù: to lodge
3. **渺小**, miǎoxiǎo: tiny
4. **因果**, yīnguǒ: cause and effect
5. **倒装**, dàozhuāng: inverted
6. **倒影**, dàoyǐng: reflection in water
7. **思绪**, sīxù: threads of thought
8. **反问句**, fǎnwènjù: rhetorical question
9. **泛**, fàn: broadly, generally
10. **名声**, míngshēng: fame, renown
11. **流离**, liúlí: wandering from place to place

练习

一、选择题

1. "细草微风岸"显示渺小，"危樯独夜舟"流露孤独，都是诗人当时的 _____ 。
   - a. 处境
   - b. 环境
   - c. 心境
   - d. 情境

2. "名岂文章著"是个 _____ 。
   - a. 问句
   - b. 反问句
   - c. 倒装句
   - d. 陈述句

3. _____ 写作会给我带来名声吗?
   - a. 怎么
   - b. 如果
   - c. 究竟
   - d. 难道

二、造句

1. 渺小　　2. 因果　　3. 倒装　　4. 思绪　　5. 名声　　6. 流离

三、中译英

1. 细草微风岸，危樯独夜舟。星垂平野阔，月涌大江流。名岂文章著？官应老病休。飘飘何所似，天地一沙鸥。

2. 第一联中有四个形容词："细"、"微"、"危"和"独"，都用得很好，既描写了风景，又透露了诗人凄凉孤独的心情。

3. "飘飘一沙鸥"既是比喻，也是对比：天地之大和沙鸥之小的对比。

四、英译中

1. In 765, Du Fu left his thatched house in Chengdu with his family and traveled down to the east in a boat.

2. Stars droop at the edge of the sky; the moon's reflection bobs on the river.

3. Du Fu didn't enjoy great fame while he was alive and became more and more famous only after his death.

五、回答题

1. 第二联的妙处在哪里?
2. 为什么诗人会觉得星星垂下来?
3. 为什么诗人会觉得月亮在涌动?
4. "名岂文章著"中的文章指的是什么?
5. 尾联中"天地一沙鸥"的形象比喻什么?

六、讨论题

1. 情景交融是中国古典诗歌的一个特色。这首诗中,除了五、六两句外,其余六句都是写景。分析这六个写景的诗句是怎么体现诗人的心情的。

七、作文

1. 题目:《杜甫的战乱诗中表现的儒家思想》

33

A Brief Introduction to Field-and-Garden Poetry
田园诗小序

江村

词汇一

1. **浣花溪**, Huànhuāxī: Washing Flowers Stream, a river in the suburb of Chengdu
2. **畔**, pàn: side, bank
3. **安顿**, āndùn: to settle down
4. **北宋**, Běi Sòng: Northern Song Dynasty (960–1126)
5. **祠**, cí: memorial temple
6. **供**, gōng: 给
7. **瞻仰**, zhānyǎng: to look upon with reverence, to pay respects
8. **公顷**, gōngqǐng: hectare
9. **栽**, zāi: to plant, to grow
10. **经营**, jīngyíng: to manage (a project or enterprise)
11. **药圃**, yàopǔ: herb plot
12. **交往**, jiāowǎng: to interact with
13. **谈心**, tánxīn: heart-to-heart talk
14. **广泛**, guǎngfàn: extensive, broad
15. **宁静**, níngjìng: peaceful, tranquil
16. **生机**, shēngjī: life, vitality
17. **蓬勃**, péngbó: vigorous
18. **美感**, měigǎn: sense of beauty
19. **抚慰**, fǔwèi: to comfort, to soothe
20. **忧患**, yōuhuàn: suffering, misery, hardship
21. **生活气息**, shēnghuó qìxī : flavor of life
22. **善于**, shànyú: to be good at
23. **捕捉**, bǔzhuō: to catch, to seize
24. **高超**, gāochāo: superb, transcendent

小序

　　杜甫在成都时，在浣花溪畔盖起了自己的茅屋—这就是有名的杜甫草堂。经过长期的漂泊，杜甫终于安顿了下来。他在这里居住了将近四年，写下了二百四十多首诗。为了纪念这位伟大的诗人，北宋以来，人们在这儿建园立祠，供人瞻仰。当年杜甫居住的茅屋早已不存在了，现在的草堂，实际上是一所优美的园林，总面积约二十公顷。

　　杜甫当年在这里栽花种草，经营药圃，和农民交往，与朋友谈心。他把这一切都写进诗里，于是在他的笔下出现了一个新的艺术天地。在这里，大自然的一切都引起他广泛的兴趣。一种和平宁静而又生机蓬勃的美感，抚慰着诗人饱经忧患的心灵。这些优美动人的田园诗，充满清新活泼的生活气息，表现出杜甫善于观察自然和捕捉艺术形象的高超本领。

练习

一、选择题

1. 经过长期的漂泊，杜甫终于 _____ 了下来。
   - a. 安定
   - b. 安排
   - c. 安顿
   - d. 安静

2. 为了纪念伟大的诗人杜甫，_____ 以来，人们在这儿建园立祠，供人瞻仰。
   - a. 唐代
   - b. 宋代
   - c. 北宋
   - d. 南宋

3. 现在的草堂，实际上是一所优美的 _____ 。
   - a. 公园
   - b. 花园
   - c. 森林
   - d. 园林

4. 大自然的一切都引起他 _____ 的兴趣。
   - a. 广大
   - b. 广泛
   - c. 广阔
   - d. 广博

5. 一种和平宁静而又生机蓬勃的美感，抚慰着诗人 _____ 的心灵。
   - a. 饱经忧患
   - b. 饱经风霜
   - c. 流离漂泊
   - d. 饥寒交迫

6. 他把这一切都写进诗里，_____ 在他的笔下出现了一个新的艺术天地。
   - a. 于是
   - b. 因此
   - c. 所以
   - d. 结果

二、造句

1. 安顿　　2. 瞻仰　　3. 经营　　4. 交往　　5. 谈心
6. 广泛　　7. 宁静　　8. 善于　　9. 高超

三、中译英

1. 他在这里栽花种草，经营药圃，和农民交往，与朋友谈心。

2. 从杜甫的田园诗中我们可以看到杜甫是个热爱生活的人。他非常珍惜浣花溪畔的和平、宁静的生活环境。

3. 田园诗是中国古代诗歌的一个流派，早期的代表人物为东晋的陶渊明，其特色在于描写农村的朴实生活和田园风光。

四、英译中

1. Du Fu built his own thatched house on the side of Washing Flowers Stream and it is now the famous Thatched Hall of Du Fu.

2. After a long period of leading a wandering life, Du Fu finally settled down.

3. Everything in nature attracted his extensive interest, and he wrote many gardens-and-fields poems.

五、回答题

1. 杜甫草堂在哪里？

2. 杜甫在草堂做些什么事？

3. 杜甫在草堂住了几年？写了多少首诗？

六、讨论题

1. 介绍一下杜甫的田园诗的写作环境和艺术特色。

七、专题研究

1. 介绍一下今日的杜甫草堂。

34

Happy About the Rain
on a Spring Night
春夜喜雨

词汇一

1. **时节**, shíjié: season
2. **当**, dāng: just at (a time)
3. **乃**, nǎi: 于是，就
4. **潜**, qián: to slip into
5. **润**, rùn: to moisten
6. **俱**, jù: 都
7. **锦官城**, Jǐnguānchén: another name for the city of Chengdu

春夜喜雨

好雨知时节，当春乃发生。
随风潜入夜，润物细无声。
野径云俱黑，江船火独明。
晓看红湿处，花重锦官城。

赏析

　　俗语说："春雨贵如油"。春雨对农作物有好处，所以杜甫会写这首"喜雨"诗。

　　首联点题，只用"知时节"三字，就将一场春雨及时降临所带给人们的喜悦生动地刻画出来。接下来三联，颔联是听，颈联是看，尾联是想。

　　因晚上下雨，诗人先是在屋中听见雨声。虽然雨很"细"，以至"无声"，但是敏感的诗人还是听到了。"润物"表达了春雨的功用，也是诗人喜悦的原因。

　　因听到了雨声，诗人到窗边观看。黑沉沉的旷野上，只有江面上闪烁着一点渔火，多么美的一幅雨夜江景图！

　　在尾联中，诗人想象明天清晨，经过一夜春雨滋润的花朵重重叠叠地开放，锦官城一定更加春意盎然了。

词汇二

1. **农作物**, nóngzuòwù: crops
2. **点题**, diǎntí: to refer to the title (of a poem, article, etc.), to bring out the theme
3. **点**, diǎn: to hint, to point out
4. **降临**, jiànglín: to arrive, to befall
5. **敏感**, mǐngǎn: sensitive
6. **功用**, gōngyòng: function
7. **黑沉沉**, hēichénchén: pitch dark
8. **旷野**, kuàngyě: wide open plain, prairie
9. **闪烁**, shǎnshuò: twinkle, glimmer, glisten
10. **滋润**, zīrùn: to moisten
11. **重重叠叠**, chóngchóng diédié: one on top of another, overlapping
12. **春意盎然**, chūnyì àngrán: brimming with spring air

练习

一、选择题

1. 首句将一场春雨及时 _____ 所带给人们的喜悦生动
地刻画出来。

      a. 滋润   b. 降临

      c. 闪烁   d. 潜入

2. 接下来三联，颔联是听，颈联是看，尾联是
_____ 。

      a. 听   b. 看

      c. 想   d. 做

3. 虽然雨很"细"， _____ "无声"，但是敏感的诗人
还是听到了。

      a. 以及   b. 以为

      c. 以至   d. 以后

4. "润物"表达了春雨的功用，也是诗人喜悦的
_____ 。

      a. 原因   b. 原则

      c. 原来   d. 来源

二、造句

1. 降临   2. 敏感   3. 功用   4. 闪烁   5. 滋润
6. 重重叠叠   7. 春意盎然

三、中译英

1. 野径云俱黑，江船火独明。
2. 诗人想象明天清晨，经过一夜春雨滋润的花朵重重叠叠
地开放。
3. 在诗歌中描写雨雪风花等自然景物的作品并不少，但是
把它们和人民的生活联系在一起的却并不多见。

四、英译中

1. Spring rain is good for crops; that is why Du Fu wrote this poem.
2. The first couplet vividly describes the joy of the poet brought by the timely arrival of the spring rain.
3. Although the rain is very light and even "silent," the sensitive poet still hears it.

五、回答题

1. 首联起了什么作用？
2. 接下来三联是怎么分工的？
3. 诗人晚上听到了什么声音？
4. 诗人看到了窗外什么景象？
5. 诗人想象明天清晨有什么样的美景？

六、讨论题

1. 这首诗题为《春夜喜雨》，但却又无一字言"喜"。请从听、看、想的顺序分析杜甫在这首诗中表达的喜悦心情。
2. 《春夜喜雨》和《茅屋为秋风所破歌》是杜甫在草堂写的两首诗。这两首诗的情绪虽然不同，但都表现了诗人对人民生活的关心。请结合这两首诗进行讨论。

七、作文

1. 题目：《喜雨》。

35

A Guest's Arrival
客至

词汇一

1. **鸥**, ōu: gull
2. **不曾**, bùcéng: 没有, never (have done something)
3. **曾**, céng: 曾经
4. **缘**, yuán: 为了，因为
5. **扫**, sǎo: to sweep
6. **蓬门**, péngmén: simple and rough door
7. **飧**, sūn: dinner, cooked food, simple food
8. **兼味**, jiānwèi: more than one dish
9. **醅**, pēi: unstrained wine
10. **隔**, gé: to separate, to be separated by
11. **篱**, lí: hedge, fence
12. **呼取**, hūqǔ: 叫来

客至

舍南舍北皆春水，但见群鸥日日来。
花径不曾缘客扫，蓬门今始为君开。
盘飧市远无兼味，尊酒家贫只旧醅。
肯与邻翁相对饮，隔篱呼取尽余杯。

赏析

　　这首诗写有客来草堂访问时杜甫的喜悦心情。

　　首联描写环境。草堂坐落在浣花溪畔，周围流水环绕，风景优美。"但见群鸥日日来"既说明诗人的住处与自然的亲近，又说明平时很少有客来访。

　　颔联写客至。"花径不曾缘客扫"接上句，说明平时来客稀少。作为对照，"蓬门今始为君开"写出有客来时诗人的兴奋心情。这两句也是"互文见义"，就是说两句放在一起，互相补充，意思才完整。因此，这两句完整的读法应是："花径不曾缘客扫，今始为君扫"；"蓬门不曾为客开，今始为君开"。

　　颈联写待客。因为"市远"和"家贫"，菜无兼味、酒只旧醅，主人似乎略有歉意。但此联也同时表达了诗人待客的诚恳和热情。

　　尾联继续写款待。诗人说，如果你愿意和邻居在一起饮酒，我就隔着篱笆叫他们共尽余杯。至此，饮酒场面之热烈，朋友情谊之真挚，都表现得非常清楚了。

词汇二

1. **坐落**, zuòluò: to be situated, to be located
2. **环绕**, huánrǎo: to surround, to encircle
3. **稀少**, xīshǎo: few, rare, scarce
4. **待客**, dàikè: to entertain guests
5. **略**, lüè: slightly, somewhat
6. **歉意**, qiànyì: apology, regret
7. **诚恳**, chéngkěn: sincere
8. **款待**, kuǎndài: to entertain, to treat
9. **篱笆**, líba: fence

练习

一、选择题

1. "互文见义" 是一种 _____ 手法。
     a. 修辞   b. 语法
     c. 结构   d. 构思

2. 因为 "市远" 和 "家贫"，菜无兼味、酒只旧醅，主人似乎略有 _____ 。
     a. 谅解   b. 解释
     c. 歉意   d. 说明

3. 至此，饮酒场面之热烈，朋友情谊之 _____ ，都表现得非常清楚了。
     a. 真实   b. 真挚
     c. 真心   d. 真正

二、造句

1. 坐落   2. 环绕   3. 稀少   4. 待客   5. 歉意
6. 诚恳   7. 款待   8. 真挚

三、中译英

1. 舍南舍北皆春水，但见群鸥日日来。花径不曾缘客扫，蓬门今始为君开。

2. 李白是 "酒仙"，杜甫也很喜欢饮酒，诗中也经常提到酒。比如，他困在长安时，"瓢弃樽无绿"；招待客人时，"尊酒家贫只旧醅"。

3. 诗的题目的作用是要告诉读者这首诗要写什么，所以一般都很平实，如《客至》、《春夜喜雨》、《新婚别》、《茅屋为秋风所破歌》。

四、英译中

1. This poem is about Du Fu's happy mood when a guest comes to visit him.

2. This line says that his residence was close to nature, and also that visitors were scarce.

3. This couplet expresses the sincerity and warmth of the poet toward his guest.

五、回答题

1. 杜甫草堂的环境怎么样?

2. 平时来访问杜甫的客人多不多? 你怎么知道?

3. 杜甫是怎么招待客人的?

六、讨论题

1. 杜甫是怎么表达有客人来访的喜悦心情的? 请举例说明。

2. 这也是首饮酒诗。比较这首诗和李白的《下终南山过斛斯山人宿置酒》所表现的饮酒方式、朋友情谊和人生态度。

七、作文

1. 写一篇题为《客至》的短文,叙述你接待客人的经历和心情。

36
River Village
江村

词汇一

1. 曲, qū: bend (of a river, etc.)
2. 燕, yàn: swallow
3. 棋局, qíjú: *weiqi* 围棋 (*go*) board; a game of *weiqi*
4. 稚, zhì: young
5. 敲, qiāo: to knock, to strike
6. 针, zhēn: needle
7. 钓钩, diàogōu: fishhook
8. 钓, diào: to angle
9. 但有, dànyǒu: 只要有
10. 禄米, lùmǐ: official salary
11. 躯, qū: the human body
12. 求, qiú: to seek, to ask for, to strive for

Field-and-Garden Poetry

江村

清江一曲抱村流，长夏江村事事幽。
自去自来堂上燕，相亲相近水中鸥。
老妻画纸为棋局，稚子敲针作钓钩。
但有故人供禄米，微躯此外更何求。

赏析

　　这首诗写杜甫在草堂的悠闲生活。第一句写环境之优美。第二句说在长长的夏日，江村中事事都很幽闲。下面领联写自然界之幽闲，颈联讲人物之幽闲。尾联表现了杜甫对这种田园生活的满足感。

　　颈联写了两个很有意思的日常生活的镜头。围棋的棋盘应是木制的，但杜甫家穷，买不起，所以他的妻子在纸上画一个。他的儿子把针敲弯做成钓鱼的钩子。虽然杜甫在草堂的生活是清贫的，但经过战乱和流亡，这种安宁的生活是很珍贵的和充满乐趣的。

词汇二

1. **悠闲**, yōuxián: leisurely and carefree
2. **幽闲**, yōuxián: secluded and quiet
3. **满足**, mǎnzú: satisfied, content
4. **感**, gǎn: feeling
5. **镜头**, jìngtóu: scene
6. **围棋**, wéiqí: *weiqi* (go), a traditional Chinese board game with black and white stones
7. **棋盘**, qípán: *weiqi* (go) board
8. **制**, zhì: to make, to manufacture
9. **弯**, wān: curved, bend
10. **流亡**, liúwáng: to be forced to leave one's native land
11. **珍贵**, zhēnguì: precious

练习

一、选择题

1. 这首诗写杜甫在草堂的 _____ 生活。
   - a. 悠闲
   - b. 清贫
   - c. 朴素
   - d. 珍贵

2. "老妻画纸为棋局" 中的棋指的是 _____ 。
   - a. 围棋
   - b. 象棋
   - c. 国际象棋
   - d. 军棋

3. 围棋的棋盘应是 _____ 制的。
   - a. 铁
   - b. 石
   - c. 木
   - d. 纸

4. 尾联表现了杜甫对这种田园生活的 _____ 感。
   - a. 兴奋
   - b. 高兴
   - c. 愉快
   - d. 满足

二、造句

1. 悠闲   2. 满足   3. 感   4. 镜头   5. 弯
6. 流亡   7. 珍贵

三、中译英

1. 自去自来堂上燕，相亲相近水中鸥。
2. 老妻画纸为棋局，稚子敲针作钓钩。
3. 杜甫草堂坐落在浣花溪畔，环境优美，杜甫在诗中多次提到。比如，他在《江村》中说："清江一曲抱村流"，在《客至》中说 "舍南舍北皆春水" 。

四、英译中

1. The third couplet presents two very interesting scenes of daily life.
2. Du Fu was poor and could not afford a *weiqi* board, so his wife drew one on paper.
3. His son made a fishhook by pounding a needle and bending it.

4. During wartime, Du Fu enjoyed and cherished this type of peaceful and simple life.

五、回答题

1. 杜甫的妻子在纸上画什么？
2. 杜甫的儿子把针敲弯做什么？
3. 为什么杜甫对这种清贫的生活很满足？

六、讨论题

1. 请你根据《江村》的诗意画一幅画，然后照着这幅画来讲解这首诗。
2. 颈联的两个日常生活的镜头很平常，但又很生动。说明这两个镜头在这首诗中的作用。
3. 杜甫的田园诗和战乱诗在写作上有什么不同的特点？

七、专题研究

1. 作一个关于围棋的报告：它的发展历史、最基本的规则以及历史上有名的围棋故事。（关键词：举棋不定、奕秋、王积薪）

Illustrations

All illustrations from Yang Yi 杨义, "Li Du Shi Xue" 李杜诗学 [The poetry of Li Bai and Du Fu], *Beijing Chubanshe* 北京出版社 (2000).

Title	【Dynasty】	Artist	Page
李太白	【清】	上官周	5
把酒问月	【清】	玄烨（康熙）	349
黄鹤楼送孟浩然	【清】	石涛	461
青莲醉酒	【清】	吴友如	91
杜工部	【清】	上官周	6
天寒翠袖薄	【清】	吴友如	596
江村	【清】	吴友如	806

Appendices:
English Translations
附录：英文翻译

Historical Background:
The An Lushan Rebellion
历史背景：安史之乱

The time of Li Bai and Du Fu was a turning point in the Tang Dynasty from grandeur to decline.

The Tang regime reached the pinnacle of its political, economic, and cultural achievements during the reign of Emperor Xuanzong. A very capable ruler when he was young, Xuanzong grew vain in his old age. He fell for Precious Concubine Yang, and afterward neglected administration and became dependent on evil advisers. In 755, a general named An Lushan mounted a rebellion against the throne in the northeastern border area. An Lushan's principal lieutenant was Shi Siming, and thus this rebellion is called the An-Shi Rebellion in Chinese history. The rebel army captured the capital Chang'an in the following year, and in a panicked haste Xuanzong fled to Sichuan. The rebellion lasted for eight years and gravely damaged Chinese society. After the rebellion was quelled, chaotic fighting broke out among warlords and the Tang Dynasty headed toward its doom.

Li Bai was eleven years older than Du Fu. This age discrepancy played an important role in their different life paths and poetic styles. Li Bai was fifty-four when the An Lushan Rebellion broke out, and he lived for seven more years afterward. Most of his poems, written before the rebellion, brim with the vitality of Tang prosperity. Du Fu was forty-three in 755, and lived for fifteen more years. In his many poems, he testified to the destructions of war and people's misfortunes.

Philosophical Background: Confucianism and Daoism
哲学背景：儒家与道家

Of the many philosophical currents that have shaped Chinese civilization over the centuries, none have been more profoundly influential than Confucianism and Daoism. Confucianism, which acknowledges Confucius as its founder, advocates morals, order, and individual contributions to society. Daoism, centered on the teachings of Laozi, focuses on individual freedom and man's status in the larger cosmic scheme. Confucians hope to establish successful careers, while Daoists want to let nature take its course. These two philosophies stand in opposition, yet are also mutually complementary.

Although Li Bai and Du Fu were good friends, they differed greatly in their outlooks on life. Li Bai was inclined toward Daoism, and dreamed of living in a free realm, forgetting the various repulsive social realities. Themes such as "life as a dream" and "making merry in a timely fashion" recur in Li Bai's poems. Du Fu was a firm Confucian scholar with high political aspirations. His poems exposed the problems of society and reflected the people's sufferings during war.

As a result, Li Bai and Du Fu were given interesting epithets: Li Bai was called the "Immortal of Poetry," and Du Fu, the "Sage of Poetry." These two appellations first of all refer to their position at the pinnacle of Chinese poetic achievements, but they also have philosophical implications. Immortality was a vital quest of Daoists and sagehood was the ultimate ideal of Confucians. Thus, an Immortal and a Sage became best friends and wrote poems of distinctly different styles, to the admiration and appreciation of later generations.

Literary Background: Poetic Form
文学背景：诗歌格律

Poetry has a long history in China. During the Tang Dynasty, poetic form matured. This form mainly includes the following elements: the number of characters and lines, rhyme, parallelism, and tonal patterns.

First of these elements is the number of characters and lines. A poem with five characters in each line is called a pentasyllabic poem. A poem with seven characters in each line is called a heptasyllabic poem. A four-line poem is called a quatrain. An eight-line poem is called regulated verse. Their combinations thus make pentasyllabic quatrains, heptasyllabic quatrains, pentasyllabic regulated verse, and heptasyllabic regulated verse. Poems with more lines and freer styles, not restricted by strict regulations, are called "ancient airs." Of course, they are also divided into pentasyllabic ancient airs and heptasyllabic ancient airs.

Classical Chinese poems are all rhymed. Rhyme is mandatory on even-numbered lines. The first line is optional, though usually rhymed.

The two middle couplets of a regulated verse must be parallel in construction. Generally speaking, two words in corresponding positions in the two lines of a couplet should be from the same semantic class. For example, a noun pairs with a noun ("heaven" with "earth"), and an adjective pairs with an adjective ("red" with "black").

More difficult are the tonal patterns. There are also four tones in ancient Chinese, but they differ from the four modern tones. The tone for each character in regulated verse is prescribed; therefore, reciting a poem provides a sense of music. This is a more complex issue. After you have studied more poems, you will gradually get a sense of this.

A Brief Biography of Li Bai
李白小传

Li Bai (701–762) had the courtesy name of Taibai. He grew up in Sichuan and showed literary talent and high aspirations at a young age. Li Bai left his hometown when he was twenty-three and traveled extensively for many years. He never took the civil service examinations as his contemporaries did, though that was the normal route to a career in government.

When he was forty-one, by friends' recommendations, Li Bai received a summons from Emperor Xuanzong which took him to the capital. He was appointed a scholar in the Hanlin Academy. In Chang'an, Li Bai drafted imperial edicts, attended the emperor at banquets and outings, and celebrated these occasions in verse. However, his unrestrained character was not compatible with court life at all, and resulted in his dismissal after less than two years. In his wanderings after that, Li Bai met Du Fu. The two of them formed a profound friendship.

In the year 755, the An Lushan Rebellion broke out. After Chang'an fell, Xuanzong fled to Sichuan. The crown prince, who was later known in history as Emperor Suzong, ascended the throne in Lingwu. Another son of Xuanzong's, Prince Yong, who led government resistance in the southeast, invited Li Bai to join his army. With patriotic fervor, Li Bai became his staff member. Suzong suspected that Prince Yong planned to contend with him for the throne, so he dispatched troops to crush the prince. Subsequently, Li Bai was arrested and was sentenced to exile in Yelang. On his way to exile in 759, Li Bai was freed by imperial amnesty in the City of Baidi. Li Bai lived a poor and wandering life in his last years and died of illness in Dangtu.

Over 1,000 of Li Bai's poems are extant. Li Bai often compared himself to the Great Roc, with full confidence in his own talents. In many of his poems, he expressed sentiments disdaining political power and social hierarchy. His poems touch readers' hearts with rich imagination, extreme exaggeration, and vivid metaphor, and are presented in a uniquely magnificent, expressive, and natural style.

A Brief Biography of Du Fu
杜甫小传

Du Fu, also known as Zimei (his courtesy name), came from a scholarly family. His grandfather Du Shenyan was also a famous poet, so Du Fu said that "Poetry is the tradition of our family." Du Fu took the civil service examinations when he was twenty-three, but failed. When he was thirty-two, Du Fu met Li Bai in Luoyang. The trajectories of these two bright stars had crossed. Although they were eleven years apart, they became lifelong friends from their first meeting. In 746, Du Fu went to Chang'an, and stayed there for ten years.

He was finally awarded a minor official position in court in 755, but soon thereafter the An Lushan Rebellion struck. When An Lushan established his bloody rule in Chang'an, Du Fu was trapped in the city. After he escaped from the rebels, he served in Suzong's court for a short period. In 759, after a long, difficult journey, Du Fu and his family settled down in Chengdu. In his later years, Du Fu left Chengdu and planned to return to Chang'an; unfortunately, he died of sickness on a shabby boat on the Xiang River.

Du Fu's impoverished and distressed life was closely tied to the social upheavals in Tang history. His poems faithfully and vividly recorded the chaos caused by war, reflecting the many momentous events of the times. Du Fu's poetry has thus been called "history in verse."

Du Fu has earned the title of the "Sage of Poetry." This honorable title is of course praise of his poetic art, but more importantly it is the recognition of the moral force of his poems. Du Fu's more than 1,400 surviving poems voice his criticisms of official corruption, concerns for the empire, and intense compassion for dispossessed people, thus manifesting the social conscience of a Confucian scholar.

Vocabulary Index
词汇索引

C

苍黄	cānghuáng	panic, same as 仓皇	29
倾耳	qīng'ěr	to bend the ear, attentively	21
层出不穷	céngchū bùqióng	to emerge one after another	12
层次	céngcì	level	20
曾	céng	曾经	35
插	chā	to stick in, to insert	30
差吏	chāilì	civil officer, clerk	28
柴	chái	firewood, brushwood	27
柴门	cháimén	door of brushwood	27
长达	chángdá	with the great length of	23
肠	cháng	gut, intestines	29
裳	cháng	bottom garment, dress	29
场面	chǎngmiàn	scene, setting	31
畅	chàng	free-flowing and unimpeded	17
朝廷	cháotíng	imperial court, imperial government	4
朝政	cháozhèng	government affairs	1
彻	chè	through	31
臣	chén	a subject under an emperor, a term for "I" used by officials when addressing the emperor	17
沉痛	chéntòng	deeply grieved	29
陈迹	chénjī	relics, vestiges	8
趁	chèn	to take advantage of	28
趁人不备	chènrén búbèi	to catch people unaware	28
称号	chēnghào	title, name	2
诚恳	chéngkěn	sincere	35
承	chéng	to continue, to carry on	26
盛	chéng	to fill	18
持续	chíxù	to continue	1
赤	chì	红	27
赤子	chìzǐ	newborn baby; common people	31
冲淡	chōngdàn	to dilute, to weaken	14
充沛	chōngpèi	plentiful, abundant	21
重	chóng	layer	15
重重叠叠	chóngchóng diédié	one on top of another, overlapping	34

崇高	chónggāo	lofty, sublime, high	22
丑恶	chǒu'è	ugly	2
初次	chūcì	第一次	12
处境	chǔjìng	(unfavorable) situation	31
川	chuān	river	13
传达	chuándá	to convey, to reveal	7
传神	chuánshén	vivid	27
传诵	chuánsòng	to be widely read, to be on everyone's lips	2
创始人	chuàngshǐrén	founder	2
炊	chuī	to cook a meal	28
垂	chuí	to droop	14
垂老	chuílǎo	with old age approaching, in declining years	23
垂柳	chuíliǔ	weeping willow	14
春意盎然	chūnyì àngrán	brimming with spring air	34
唇	chún	lip	31
词类	cílèi	parts of speech (such as noun, verb, etc.)	3
祠	cí	memorial temple	33
辞	cí	告别	14
次年	cìnián	following year	1
刺激	cìjī	to stimulate	17
匆忙	cōngmáng	hastily, hurriedly	29
从	cóng	to follow, to join	16
从而	cóng'ér	thus, thereby	10
翠	cuì	emerald green, bluish green	30
翠微	cuìwēi	green mountain side	20
存	cún	to exist	25
错迕	cuòwù	disorderly and adverse	29

D

搭配	dāpèi	to match up, to coordinate	3
大局	dàjú	overall situation	29
大赦	dàshè	amnesty	4
大肆	dàsì	without restraint, wantonly	26
大致	dàzhì	generally, roughly	3

待客	dàikè	to entertain guests	35
逮捕	dàibǔ	to arrest	4
丹	dān	红	10
单纯	dānchún	simple, pure	6
但使	dànshǐ	只要	18
但有	dànyǒu	只要有	36
淡泊	dànbó	to lead a tranquil life without worldly desires	20
淡化	dànhuà	to lighten, to lessen	5
当	dāng	应该	10
当	dāng	just at (a time)	34
捣	dǎo	to pound with a pestle	10
倒影	dàoyǐng	reflection in water	32
倒装	dàozhuāng	inverted	32
盗	dào	thief, robber	31
道家	Dàojiā	Daoism (Taoism)	2
得	dé	能	28
得意	déyì	pleased with oneself or one's situation	21
登	dēng	to ascend, to board	14
登前途	dēng qiántú	to start off on a journey, to set out	28
抵	dǐ	to be equal to	26
地势	dìshì	topography, terrain	15
第一人称	dìyī rénchēng	the first person	29
点	diǎn	to hint, to point out	34
点明	diǎnmíng	to point out	9
点题	diǎntí	to refer to the title (of a poem, article, etc.), to bring out the theme	34
典故	diǎngù	allusion	25
典型	diǎnxíng	model, typical example	23
钓	diào	to angle	36
钓钩	diàogōu	fishhook	36
顶峰	dǐngfēng	peak	1
动	dòng	often, easily	30
动荡	dòngdàng	turbulence, upheaval	22
动态	dòngtài	dynamic state	13
动作	dòngzuò	action, movement	19
冻	dòng	to freeze, to feel very cold	31

斗	dǒu	goblet, drinking vessel	17
都会	dūhuì	metropolis	14
渡	dù	to cross (a river, the sea, etc.)	16
端	duān	end	5
短语	duǎnyǔ	phrase	15
短暂	duǎnzàn	short duration, transience	5
断	duàn	severed, broken	12
对比	duìbǐ	contrast	8
对立	duìlì	in opposition, conflicting	2
对仗	duìzhàng	parallelism (in poetry)	3
咄咄怪事	duōduō guàishì	what a queer story, what a strange phenomenon	25

E

俄顷	éqǐng	in a moment	31
恶卧	èwò	to not sleep peacefully	31
儿	ér	小孩	21
尔	ěr	你	21

F

发	fā	to emit, to radiate	10
发	fā	出发	15
发愁	fāchóu	to worry	25
发挥	fāhuī	to develop (an idea, a theme, etc.), to elaborate	26
发扬	fāyáng	to develop, to carry on	31
翻滚	fāngǔn	to roll, to tumble	12
烦恼	fánnǎo	vexation, worries	5
繁	fán	numerous, abundant	14
繁华	fánhuá	flourishing	14
反	fǎn	on the contrary, instead	29
反衬	fǎnchèn	to set off by contrast, to serve as a foil to	19

反而	fǎn'ér	on the contrary, instead	12
反问句	fǎnwènjù	rhetorical question	32
返	fǎn	回	21
泛	fàn	broadly, generally	32
方	fāng	刚	28
飞跃	fēiyuè	to leap	8
废墟	fèixū	ruins	26
分明	fēnmíng	clear, distinct	20
风格	fēnggé	style	1
烽火	fēnghuǒ	beacon fire	26
否定	fǒudìng	to negate, to renounce	4
夫婿	fūxù	husband	30
伏笔	fúbǐ	foreshadowing (in writing)	15
拂	fú	to whisk	20
服役	fúyì	to enlist in the army	28
俘虏	fúlǔ	to capture, to take prisoner	24
抚慰	fǔwèi	to comfort, to soothe	33
腐败	fǔbài	corruption	22
附	fù	带, (to ask someone) to take, to attach to	28
赴	fù	去，到	29
复	fù	再	8
复杂	fùzá	complicated, complex	3
副手	fùshǒu	lieutenant, assistant	1
富有	fùyǒu	rich in, full of	12
赋予	fùyǔ	to bestow	11

G

盖	gài	to build (a house)	31
概括	gàikuò	summary	28
甘愿	gānyuàn	willingly	31
感	gǎn	feeling	36
感觉	gǎnjué	perception, feeling	7
感伤	gǎnshāng	sad, sentimental	9

光艳	guāngyàn	bright and colorful	18
光阴	guāngyīn	time	21
广泛	guǎngfàn	extensive, broad	33
归	guī	(said of a woman) marriage	29
闺	guī	女子的卧室	24
规定	guīdìng	to prescribe, to formulate	3
轨迹	guǐjī	orbit, trajectory	22
鬼	guǐ	ghost	25
贵妃	guìfēi	Precious Concubine (a high-ranking imperial concubine)	1
裹	guǒ	to bind, to wrap	31
过	guò	经过	20

H

海楼	hǎilóu	mirage	16
含义	hányì	meaning, implication	2
寒士	hánshì	a poor scholar	31
颔	hàn	the chin, the jaws	16
颔联	hànlián	律诗的第二联	16
号	háo	to howl, to yell	31
豪放	háofàng	vigorous and unrestrained	18
合昏	héhūn	also called 夜合花, which opens in the morning and closes in the evening	30
何不	hébù	为什么不	21
何为	héwèi	为什么	21
何以	héyǐ	拿什么，怎么能	29
何由	héyóu	怎么才能	31
河	hé	银河 (the Milky Way)	20
黑沉沉	hēichénchén	pitch dark	34
痕	hén	mark, trace	24
恨	hèn	to hate, to resent	26
横	héng	to permeate	20
横跨	héngkuà	to stretch over or across	8
红妆	hóngzhuāng	makeup	29

呼	hū	to call	17
呼取	hūqǔ	叫来	35
呼声	hūshēng	voice (of a strong opinion)	31
呼应	hūyìng	to echo each other, to work in concert with	15
壶	hú	pot, kettle	19
琥珀	hǔpò	amber	18
花瓣	huābàn	petal	26
怀	huái	to cherish, to keep in mind	7
怀	huái	胸怀, bosom, mind	20
怀才不遇	huáicái búyù	to have talent but no opportunity to use it	21
怀古	huáigǔ	to meditate on the past	8
欢颜	huānyán	happy (face)	31
还	huán	返回	15
环绕	huánrǎo	to surround, to encircle	35
鬟	huán	bun of hair	24
幻想	huànxiǎng	to cherish illusions, to imagine	2
荒	huāng	desolate	8
皇妃	huángfēi	imperial concubine	7
皇后	huánghòu	empress	7
皇位	huángwèi	the throne	4
幌	huǎng	curtain	24
挥	huī	to wave, to wield	20
辉	huī	light, brilliance	10
辉煌	huīhuáng	splendid and majestic	8
回	huí	whirling	25
回旋	huíxuán	to circle round, to whirl (of water)	12
洄	huí	to whirl (of water)	12
会须	huìxū	应当	21
浑	hún	简直、几乎	26
混战	hùnzhàn	tangled warfare	1
活力	huólì	vigor, vitality	11
豁达	huòdá	open-minded, carefree	19

J

降临	jiànglín	to arrive, to befall	34
交	jiāo	juncture, junction	12
交叉	jiāochā	to intersect, to cross	22
交代	jiāodài	to explain, to make clear	14
交欢	jiāohuān	to get along with each other happily	19
交流	jiāoliú	to communicate, to exchange	19
交往	jiāowǎng	to interact with	33
浇	jiāo	to pour, to sprinkle, to irrigate	17
娇	jiāo	delicate, pampered	31
焦	jiāo	burnt	31
角度	jiǎodù	angle, perspective	12
皎洁	jiǎojié	(of moonlight) white and clear	5
阶	jiē	steps, stairs	7
皆	jiē	都	10
揭露	jiēlù	to unmask, to expose	2
嗟	jiē	to sigh, to lament	29
结	jié	to form, to congeal	16
结发	jiéfà	usually, 结发夫妻: husband and wife of the first marriage	29
解	jiě	懂	19
借酒浇愁	jièjiǔjiāochóu	to wash away one's worries with wine	17
今朝	jīnzhāo	今天	17
锦	jǐn	brocade	14
尽	jìn	exhausted, finished	6
尽情	jìnqíng	to one's heart's content	18
进酒	jìnjiǔ	to fill the wine cup for a guest and urge him to drink it up	21
浸泡	jìnpào	to soak, to immerse	18
经营	jīngyíng	to manage (a project or enterprise)	33
荆扉	jīngfēi	door of brushwood—poor household	20
惊喜交集	jīngxǐ jiāojí	mixed feelings of surprise and joy	27
惊讶	jīngyà	surprising	27
晶莹	jīngyíng	glittering and crystal-clear	5
颈	jǐng	neck	16
颈联	jǐnglián	律诗的第三联	16
景观	jǐngguān	scene, landscape	8

径	jìng	小路	20
径须	jìngxū	to do anything as one wishes, by all means	21
境界	jìngjiè	state, realm	2
静态	jìngtài	static state	13
镜头	jìngtóu	scene	36
迥异	jiǒngyì	distinctly different	2
酒坛	jiǔtán	wine jug	25
酒意	jiǔyì	tipsy feeling	17
掬	jū	to hold with both hands, a double handful	30
局面	júmiàn	situation, phase	1
举	jǔ	to lift, to raise	6
俱	jù	都	34
卷	juǎn	to sweep off	31
罥	juàn	to entwine, to wind	31
决	jué	to breach, to burst	12
绝	jué	to be finished	28
绝代	juédài	当代最好的	30
绝句	juéjù	quatrain, a poem of four lines	3
军阀	jūnfá	warlord	1
君	jūn	you (used in addressing a male in formal speech)	20

K

开怀畅饮	kāihuái chàngyǐn	to drink to one's heart's content	20
开阔	kāikuò	broad, wide	11
科举	kējǔ	civil service examinations (in imperial times)	4
渴望	kěwàng	to have thirst for, to yearn for	23
刻画	kèhuà	to depict, to portray	29
客	kè	to live or stay in a strange land	18
肯定	kěndìng	to affirm	22
空间	kōngjiān	space	8
恐	kǒng	probably, perhaps (with reference to an unpleasant fact)	29
控诉	kòngsù	to denounce, to condemn	29

扣		kòu	to refer to, to button up	26
苦况		kǔkuàng	miserable situation	31
酷		kù	cruel	28
夸张		kuāzhāng	exaggeration	4
款待		kuǎndài	to entertain, to treat	35
狂放		kuángfàng	unrestrained (character)	4
旷野		kuàngyě	wide open plain, prairie	34
困		kùn	to be under siege, to be trapped	22
困境		kùnjìng	difficult situation	28
阔		kuò	wide, broad, vast	32

L

阑		lán	late	27
览		lǎn	to look at, to see, to view	8
狼狈		lángbèi	in a difficult, awkward position	31
朗		lǎng	bright	5
朗诵		lǎngsòng	to recite (a poem, etc.)	3
老翁		lǎowēng	old man	25
乐于		lèyú	to be happy to, to take delight in	18
类型		lèixíng	type, mode	23
冷清		lěngqīng	cold and deserted	19
篱		lí	hedge, fence	35
篱笆		líba	fence	35
里		lǐ	lining	31
理		lǐ	to manage, to run	1
立足点		lìzúdiǎn	foothold, standpoint	12
吏		lì	civil officer, clerk	23
帘		lián	curtain, blinds	7
怜		lián	爱	16
联		lián	(poetic) couplet	3
联想		liánxiǎng	to think of in connection (with the aforementioned)	31
练		liàn	white silk	13
良家子		liángjiāzǐ	children of good parentage	30

良心	liángxīn	conscience	22
谅解	liàngjiě	understanding, forgiveness	28
聊	liáo	tentatively, lightly	20
裂	liè	to split open	31
临	lín	to approach, to reach	10
玲珑	línglóng	bright and exquisite	7
凌晨	língchéng	wee hours of the morning	20
菱	líng	water chestnut	8
零乱	língluàn	helter-skelter	19
零落	língluò	withered and fallen	30
流放	liúfàng	exile	4
流离	liúlí	wandering from place to place	32
流露	liúlù	to reveal, to show unintentionally	15
流派	liúpài	schools (of thought, art, etc.)	2
流亡	liúwáng	to be forced to leave one's native land	36
庐	lú	hut, cottage	31
禄米	lùmǐ	official salary	36
露	lù	dew	7
沦陷区	lúnxiànqū	enemy-occupied area	24
论	lùn	to discuss, to talk about	30
罗	luó	silk gauze	7
萝	luó	a kind of creeping plant	20
律诗	lùshī	regulated verse	3
略	lüè	slightly, somewhat	35

M

麻	má	hemp	29
满足	mǎnzú	satisfied, content	36
漫游	mànyóu	roaming, wandering	4
蔓	màn	tendril, creeper	29
矛盾	máodùn	contradictory, contradiction	2
茅屋	máowū	thatched house	23
美感	měigǎn	sense of beauty	33
蒙受	méngshòu	to suffer, to sustain	26

梦寐	mèngmèi	dream	27
密切	mìqiè	close, inseparable	22
描绘	miǎo(2)huì	to depict, to describe	1
渺小	miǎoxiǎo	tiny	32
邈	miǎo	远	19
蔑视	mièshì	to disdain	4
民不聊生	mínbù liáoshēng	people have no means of livelihood	28
敏感	mǐngǎn	sensitive	34
名声	míngshēng	fame, renown	32
明明	míngmíng	obviously	24
命运	mìngyùn	destiny, fate	28
末	mò	end	29
没	mò	to sink, to be submerged, to disappear	10
莫	mò	不要	21
漠漠	mòmò	misty and vast	31
目送	mùsòng	to follow with the eyes	14
暮	mù	dusk, evening, sunset	20
暮春	mùchūn	late spring	9
幕僚	mùliáo	close aide (to someone in high office)	4

N

那	nǎ	哪	30
乃	nǎi	于是，就	34
男	nán	儿子	28
难民	nànmín	refugee	24
拟人	nǐrén	personification	16
宁静	níngjìng	peaceful, tranquil	33
宁	nìng	难道	10
农历	nónglì	Chinese lunar calendar	14
农作物	nóngzuòwù	crops	34
浓	nóng	dense, thick, great, strong	20
孥	nú	children	27
怒	nù	angry	28

O

鸥	ōu	gull	35
偶然	ǒurán	fortuitous, by chance	27

P

徘徊	páihuái	to pace back and forth, to hesitate	19
攀	pān	to climb	5
判	pàn	to sentence	4
叛军	pànjūn	rebellious army	1
畔	pàn	side, bank	33
磅礴	pángbó	extensive, majestic	13
醅	pēi	unstrained wine	35
烹	pēng	to cook, to boil	21
蓬	péng	fleabane	29
蓬勃	péngbó	vigorous	33
蓬门	péngmén	simple and rough door	35
鹏	péng	roc (an enormous, mythical bird of prey)	4
批判	pīpàn	to criticize	22
偏偏	piānpiān	(an adverb indicating a sense of obstinate contrariness)	24
漂泊	piāobó	to lead a wandering life	4
飘	piāo	to flutter	32
飘荡	piāodàng	to drift about	27
飘零	piāolíng	leaves falling; people leading a wandering life	9
飘散	piāosàn	drifting and scattering	9
飘逸	piāoyì	graceful and natural	4
瓢	piáo	ladle (often made of a dried gourd)	25
贫	pín	穷	29
品质	pǐnzhì	character, quality	29
平定	píngdìng	to suppress, to put down (a rebellion)	1
平和	pínghé	peaceful, gentle	20
平叛	píngpàn	平定叛乱, to suppress a rebellion	23
平坦	píngtǎn	(of land, etc.) level, even, smooth	16

凭借	píngjiè	to rely on, to depend on	17
迫	pò	to press	29
迫切	pòqiè	urgent	15
破碎	pòsuì	tattered, broken	26
扑鼻	pūbí	to come suddenly to one's nostrils (as a strong smell)	18
朴素	pǔsù	simple, plain	27
瀑布	pùbù	waterfall	11

Q

妻小	qīxiǎo	wife and children	24
凄凉	qīliáng	sad, miserable	24
栖	qī	to perch, to dwell, to stay	10
期	qī	to expect, to await, to look forward to	19
欺	qī	to bully, to take advantage of	31
其	qí	他 (她、它)，他的 (她的、它的)	18
其实	qíshi	actually	15
棋局	qíjú	weiqi 围棋 (go) board; a game of weiqi	36
棋盘	qípán	weiqi (go) board	36
岂	qǐ	难道	32
起兵	qǐbīng	to rise in arms, to start military action	1
气氛	qìfēn	atmosphere	9
气势	qìshì	imposing manner, momentum	12
弃	qì	to throw away, to discard	25
泣	qì	低声哭	28
契机	qìjī	turning point, juncture	10
憩	qì	rest	20
千金	qiānjīn	一千斤黄金，形容非常贵重的东西	21
牵	qiān	to pull	30
前	qián	走上前去	28
潜	qián	to slip into	34
歉意	qiànyì	apology, regret	35
千古	qiāngǔ	through the ages	2

将	qiāng	请	21
强调	qiángdiào	to emphasize	2
樯	qiáng	mast	32
抢掠	qiǎnglüè	to loot, to sack	26
敲	qiāo	to knock, to strike	36
巧妙	qiǎomiào	ingenious, clever	16
且	qiě	for the time being, for the moment	21
妾	qiè	concubine (in old China, a term used by a wife to refer to herself when speaking to her husband)	29
侵	qīn	to invade, to erode	7
衾	qīn	quilt	31
轻薄	qīngbó	frivolous, philandering	30
轻薄儿	qīngbó'ér	a frivolous youngster, a coxcomb	30
轻快	qīngkuài	brisk, lively, light-hearted	15
倾向	qīngxiàng	to be inclined to, to prefer	2
清净	qīngjìng	peaceful and quiet	5
清冷	qīnglěng	chilly and deserted	7
清贫	qīngpín	poor and virtuous	30
清新	qīngxīn	pure and fresh	6
情景交融	qíngjǐng jiāoróng	fuse scene with feeling (in writing)	7
情态	qíngtài	spirit and manner	27
情绪	qíngxù	feeling, mood, sentiment	12
求	qiú	to seek, to ask for, to strive for	36
裘	qiú	皮衣	21
曲	qū	bend (of a river, etc.)	36
躯	qū	the human body	36
泉	quán	spring	30
权贵	quánguì	powerful high officials	4
却	què	but, yet	6
雀	què	sparrow	27
阙	què	palace	10

R

染	rǎn	to dye, to contaminate	5
人生观	rénshēngguān	outlook on life	2
人事	rénshì	human affairs	29
忍	rěn	to be hardhearted enough to	31
仍	réng	still, yet	16
日脚	rìjiǎo	sun beams radiating through the clouds	27
戎行	rónghángg	军队	29
儒家	Rújiā	Confucianism	2
襦	rú	a short coat, a short top garment	29
乳	rǔ	奶, breast	28
润	rùn	to moisten	34
若	ruò	象	10

S

洒	sǎ	to spray	31
丧乱	sāngluàn	disturbance, turmoil	31
丧败	sàngbài	失败	30
搔	sāo	to scratch	26
扫	sǎo	to sweep	35
杀戮	shālù	massacre, slaughter	30
沙鸥	shāōu	海鸥, sea gull	32
厦	shà	a tall building	31
山人	shānrén	hermit, recluse	20
闪烁	shǎnshuò	twinkle, glimmer, glisten	34
善于	shànyú	to be good at	33
尚	shàng	尚且, even	30
梢	shāo	the tip of a branch	31
身	shēn	身分, status, identity	29
深沉	shēnchén	deep, somber	8
深刻	shēnkè	deep, profound	30
深入浅出	shēnrù qiǎnchū	to explain the profound in simple terms	10

深挚	shēnzhì	deep and sincere	29
神秘	shénmì	mysterious	10
神奇	shénqí	magical, miraculous	5
神情	shénqíng	expression	20
生动	shēngdòng	lively, vividly	6
生活气息	shēnghuó qìxī	flavor of life	33
生机	shēngjī	life, vitality	33
生离死别	shēnglí sǐbié	to part forever	29
声调	shēngdiào	tones	3
圣	shèng	sage	2
胜	shèng	to be equal or up to (a certain task)	26
盛	shèng	flourishing, prosperous	1
失望	shīwàng	disappointed	7
施	shī	to use, to apply	29
时节	shíjié	season	34
史诗	shǐshī	epic	23
驶	shǐ	to sail, to drive	12
世情	shìqíng	human feelings	30
事	shì	从事, to be engaged in (a career)	29
侍婢	shìbì	maidservant	30
侍从	shìcóng	to follow and to serve	4
视觉	shìjué	visual sense, vision	9
视野	shìyě	field of vision	16
拭	shì	to wipe	27
逝	shì	to pass, to die	21
誓	shì	to vow, to swear	29
手法	shǒufǎ	(artistic) skill, technique	7
首	shǒu	head, first	9
首联	shǒulián	律诗的第一联	16
书	shū	信	28
书	shū	写	32
书空	shūkōng	用手指在空中写字	25
书香门第	shūxiāng méndì	a scholar's family	22
抒发	shūfā	to express (poetically)	8
抒写	shūxiě	to express, to describe	24

天子	tiānzǐ	Son of Heaven, the emperor	17
田家	tiánjiā	farmer's family	20
听觉	tīngjué	sense of hearing	9
童稚	tóngzhì	children	20
偷生	tōushēng	to live an ignoble life	28
投 (宿)	tóusù	to seek temporary lodging	28
透过	tòuguò	through	7
突兀	tūwù	sudden	31
途经	tújīng	路过，经过	15
徒	tú	merely, in vain	19
兔	tù	rabbit, hare	10
菟丝	tùsī	dodder	29
团聚	tuánjù	reunion	24
团圆	tuányuán	family reunion	6
推荐	tuījiàn	to recommend	4

W

弯	wān	curved, bend	36
完	wán	complete, intact	28
完备	wánbèi	complete	3
顽童	wántóng	naughty child	31
万古	wàngǔ	through the ages	21
危	wēi	高	32
围棋	wéiqí	*weiqi* (*go*), a traditional Chinese board game with black and white stones	36
惟	wéi	只	8
唯	wéi	只	10
尾	wěi	tail	16
尾联	wěilián	律诗的第四联	16
尾声	wěishēng	epilogue, ending, (music) coda	28
未	wèi	还没有	29
位置	wèizhi	place, position	16
尉	wèi	a military officer	9
闻	wén	听，听到	9

晓	xiǎo	dawn	10
歇	xiē	停歇, to stop	30
携	xié	to hold somebody by the hand	20
携带	xiédài	to take along	24
心境	xīnjìng	state of mind, mood	20
心灵	xīnlíng	heart, soul	5
新人	xīnrén	a new wife (in reference to the original wife)	30
行	xíng	an ancient poetic form	5
形成	xíngchéng	to take shape, to form	13
形势	xíngshì	situation	29
雄奇	xióngqí	magnificent and marvelous	4
雄伟	xióngwěi	grand, magnificent	11
雄心壮志	xióngxīn zhuàngzhì	lofty aspirations	4
休	xiū	to stop, to cease	32
修	xiū	长	30
修辞	xiūcí	rhetoric	20
秀丽	xiùlì	beautiful and graceful	11
须	xū	must	19
虚	xū	空、透明	24
嘘唏	xūxī	to sob	27
叙事诗	xùshìshī	narrative poem	27
悬	xuán	to hang	8
学派	xuépài	schools (of learning, thought)	2
谑	xuè	to make jokes	21

Y

押送	yāsòng	to send under escort or guard	24
押韵	yāyùn	to rhyme	3
烟花	yānhuā	a description of the spring scene with flowers blooming	14
言	yán	说	21
岩	yán	rock, cliff	12
宴游	yànyóu	宴会和游览	4

应征	yìngzhēng	to be recruited	29
永恒	yǒnghéng	eternity	5
咏	yǒng	to chant, to recite (a poem)	5
涌	yǒng	to gush, to surge, to bob	32
忧患	yōuhuàn	suffering, misery, hardship	33
忧虑	yōulǜ	worry, anxiety	23
幽	yōu	deep and secluded	20
幽闲	yōuxián	secluded and quiet	36
幽咽	yōuyè	低声哭泣	28
悠闲	yōuxián	leisurely and carefree	36
由来	yóulái	origin	9
犹	yóu	还	28
于	yú	在	2
宇宙	yǔzhòu	universe, cosmos	2
玉	yù	jade	24
姬	yù	老年妇人	28
郁金香	yùjīnxiāng	tulip	18
欲	yù	要	26
寓	yù	to lodge	32
御	yù	to resist, to keep out	30
逾	yù	to pass over, to scale (a wall)	28
御寒	yùhán	to keep out the cold	30
鸳鸯	yuānyang	Mandarin ducks (symbolic of an affectionate couple)	30
源远流长	yuányuǎn liúcháng	a distant source and a long stream— of long standing, well-established	3
猿	yuán	gibbon	15
缘	yuán	为了，因为	35
苑	yuàn	garden, park	8
怨	yuàn	resentment, grievance	7
乐感	yuègǎn	musical feeling	3
云	yún	说	30
云汉	yúnhàn	the Milky Way	19
云鬟	yúnhuán	beautiful and thick hair (like a cloud)	24

Z

栽	zāi	to plant, to grow	33
宰	zǎi	to slaughter, to butcher	21
簪	zān	hairpin	26
赞 扬	zànyáng	to paise, to speak highly of	22
遭	zāo	to meet with (disaster, misfortune)	27
遭 遇	zāoyù	(bitter) experience	23
早	zǎo	早上	15
造 反	zàofǎn	to rebel, to revolt	1
噪	zào	to chirp	27
燥	zào	dry	31
贼	zéi	thief	31
摘	zhāi	to pick, to pluck	30
沾	zhān	to moisten, to wet	7
瞻 仰	zhānyǎng	to look upon with reverence, to pay respects	33
战 局	zhànjú	war situation/state	23
战 役	zhànyì	campaign, battle	23
朝	zhāo	早上	15
诏 书	zhàoshū	imperial edict	4
照 样	zhàoyàng	all the same, as before	26
照 耀	zhàoyào	to shine on	13
哲 理	zhélǐ	philosophical theory, philosophy	10
针	zhēn	needle	36
珍 贵	zhēnguì	precious	36
真 挚	zhēnzhì	sincere, cordial	27
征	zhēng	to journey	23
征 夫	zhēngfū	战士, soldier	29
征 召	zhēngzhào	to summon	4
峥 嵘	zhēngróng	lofty and steep	27
之	zhī	him, her, it	10
之	zhī	去、到	14
支 配	zhīpèi	to control, to dominate	18
只 今	zhǐjīn	now	8
至	zhì	到	27
制	zhì	to make, to manufacture	36

致	zhì	to achieve, to attain	29
致词	zhìcí	讲话	28
置	zhì	to set	20
稚	zhì	young	36
中肠	zhōngcháng	deep inside	29
忠实	zhōngshí	faithful	22
终年	zhōngnián	all year round	30
终身	zhōngshēn	life-long	22
钟	zhōng	bell	21
钟情	zhōngqíng	to be deeply in love	5
重用	zhòngyòng	to put somebody in an important position	1
舟	zhōu	船	14
周	zhōu	circumference, circuit	31
珠	zhū	pearl	30
烛	zhú	candle	27
主人公	zhǔréngōng	protagonist	29
主题	zhǔtí	theme	2
注入	zhùrù	to pour into, to instill, to infuse	11
著	zhù	outstanding, notable, famed	32
转折	zhuǎnzhé	a turn in the course of events	1
转烛	zhuǎnzhú	(a metaphor for quick changes)	30
馔	zhuàn	to eat and drink	21
馔玉	zhuànyù	to have delicious and sumptuous food	21
壮丽	zhuànglì	beautiful and majestic	11
追求	zhuīqiú	to seek, to pursue	2
追溯	zhuīsù	to trace back	8
浊	zhuó	turbid, muddy	30
酌	zhuó	to pour out wine, to drink	19
着眼	zhuóyǎn	to pay attention to	2
着重	zhuózhòng	to emphasize	29
姿态	zītài	posture	11
滋润	zīrùn	to moisten	34
子规	zǐguī	cuckoo	9
紫	zǐ	purple	13
字	zì	courtesy name	4
字里行间	zìlǐ hángjiān	between the lines	12

Proper Names Index
专名索引

楚江	Chǔjiāng	referring to this particular portion of the Yangtze River, since Dangtu was in the State of Chu 楚 during the Warring States 战国 period (403–221 BCE)	12
春秋	Chūnqiū	the Spring and Autumn Period (770–476 BCE)	8

D

丹丘生	Dānqiū shēng	Yuán Dānqiū 元丹丘, 李白的朋友 (fl. 728–ca. 750)	21
当涂	Dāngtú	in Anhui 安徽 Province	4
杜审言	Dù Shěnyán	唐朝诗人 (ca. 645–ca. 708)	22

F

夫差	Fūchāi	King of Wu (d. 473 BCE)	8
鄜州	Fūzhōu	a city in today's Shaanxi Province	24

G

关中	Guānzhōng	Chang'an area	30
广陵	Guǎnglíng	today's Yangzhou 扬州, in Jiangsu Province	14

H

翰林院	Hànlín Yuàn	Hanlin Academy (where literary and artistic talents were lodged)	4
河阳	Héyáng	a city in today's Henan Province	28
斛斯	húsī	复姓 (两个字的姓)	20
浣花溪	Huànhuāxī	Washing Flowers Stream, a river in the suburb of Chengdu	33
黄鹤楼	Huánghèlóu	the Yellow Crane Tower, in today's Wuhan 武汉 City of Hubei 湖北 Province	14

J

江陵	Jiānglíng	a city in Hubei Province	15
江苏	Jiāngsū	Jiangsu Province	8
晋朝	Jìncháo	the Jin Dynasty (265–420)	25
荆门	Jīngmén	a mountain in Hubei Province	16
九天	jiǔtiān	the Ninth Heaven, the highest level of Heaven	13

K

孔子	Kǒngzi	Confucius (551–479 BCE)	2

L

兰陵	Lánlíng	a city in today's Shangdong 山东 Province, known for its wine-making	18
老子	Lǎozi	Laozi	2
灵武	Língwǔ	in Ningxia 宁夏 Hui Autonomous Region	4
龙标	Lóngbiāo	a city in today's Hunan 湖南 Province	9
庐山	Lúshān	Mount Lu, in Jiangxi 江西 Province	11
洛阳	Luòyáng	a city in Henan 河南 Province	22

M

孟浩然	Mèng Hàorán	Tang poet (689–ca. 740)	14

P

平乐	Pínglè	Pingle Temple, where Cao Zhi held a lavish banquet	21

Q

S

T

W

Proper Names Index

X

Y

Z